Connected

Connected

A Reluctant Case for the Necessity
of the Church

Robert G. Moss

WIPF & STOCK · Eugene, Oregon

CONNECTED
A Reluctant Case for the Necessity of the Church

Wipf & Stock
An Imprint of Wipf and Stock Publishers
199 W. 8th Ave., Suite 3
Eugene, OR 97401

www.wipfandstock.com

PAPERBACK ISBN: 979-8-3852-0610-0
HARDCOVER ISBN: 979-8-3852-0611-7
EBOOK ISBN: 979-8-3852-0612-4

VERSION NUMBER 04/11/24

Contents

Introduction

THE ORIGINAL WORKING TITLE for this book was "Despite All Evidence to the Contrary by Virtually Everyone Everywhere, the Church May Not Completely Suck." I chose not to use it, primarily because it's too long. There may be more legitimate literary reasons, but that title does come very close to conveying my intent in writing this. The church as we know it in America is broken. It has been for a long time. So long, in fact, that we generally consider this broken state to be normal, the way it always was, and the way it was meant to be. Our culture and, if I may be so bold, God are telling us otherwise. It's trendy these days to call for the demise of the church, and thousands more are abandoning it every week if they were ever part of it at all. I find it hard to blame them. Who wants to be part of an institution that sustains itself largely through judgment and self-righteousness? For an organization purporting to be about love, grace, and compassion in the name of Jesus, the church has missed the mark in countless ways. And yet . . .

Concurring with many who find the church pointless, if not downright harmful, this book is my attempt to explain why it should nonetheless exist. Despite a growing number of Americans disregarding the church, its life is just as critical to the world in this moment as it has ever been. Not in its present form, certainly, but it must exist. To fulfill its purpose, there are drastic and systemic changes that must take place, and, to be honest, I'm not sure the church is up for that. While in this book I will try to validate the need for the church, I am not entirely optimistic that the church as we know it will ever get there.

The Christian church's foundational identity was simply people who followed the way of Jesus of Nazareth. In fact, its adherents were first referred to as "people of the Way." Since then, it has been articulated as the universal body of Christ, the "one holy catholic and apostolic church," as expressed in the Nicene Creed.[1] The apostle Paul tried to convey what he meant by the church when he wrote, "Because there is one bread, we who are many are one body, for we all partake of the one bread" (1 Corinthians 10:17). Perhaps because that is rather hard to grasp, he tried again: "For as in one body we have many members, and not all the members have the same function, so we, who are many, are one body in Christ, and individually we are members one of another" (Romans 12:4–5). Apparently from its beginning the church has had something to do with community gathered for a purpose. At least Paul thought so.

About fifteen centuries later, Martin Luther tried his hand at defining the church. He wrote about it as a community centered on what he referred to as "true faith" and gathered by the Holy Spirit:

> I believe that by my own understanding or strength I cannot believe in Jesus Christ my Lord or come to him, but instead the Holy Spirit has called me through the gospel, enlightened me with [the Spirit's] gifts, made me holy and kept me in the true faith, just as [the Spirit] calls, gathers, enlightens, and makes holy the whole Christian church on earth and keeps it with Jesus Christ in the one common, true faith.[2]

It's likely that throughout its existence people have always thought they understood what the church is and why it is. I'm not sure there's ever been full agreement on it. Still today there are debates raging across church lines about what is required for one to be part of the Christian church. Can one be part of the body if one isn't baptized correctly (or at all)? Or if one questions the virgin birth of Jesus? Or doubts the factual, historic truth of Christ's miracles as

1. "Nicene Creed," 104.
2. Luther, "Explanation," 31.

2

recorded in the Gospels? Or isn't convinced of the literal, physical resurrection of Jesus from the dead? Can someone be part of the church if they feel a need to cross their fingers when reciting parts of the Apostles' Creed on Sunday morning?

For most of Christian history, the church has thought of itself as a particular institution that adheres to certain beliefs and doctrines that promote a lifestyle pleasing to God and assure its members of eternal life in heaven. Something along those lines, anyway. Belong to the church, go to heaven when you die. There have been various iterations of this theme, but it usually falls somewhere in that vicinity. Ultimately, the church itself has declared who is visibly in and who is out, and therefore who is guaranteed to live in joy and happiness forever and, not coincidentally, who will suffer in eternal agony. That's a lot of power. It's also a lot of bunk. It really has very little, if anything, to do with the actual identity of the church.

The church described in this book is not merely a gathering of the faithful, not a collection of individuals who believe certain things, nor is it those who live a subjectively approved lifestyle. Yet for the purposes of this book, we need to articulate some boundaries, as perforated as they may (and ought to) be, around who and what is "the church."

Within these chapters, the definition of the church I will be using hearkens back to its origins: *the community claiming to follow Jesus of Nazareth.* Notice this definition doesn't mention any particular beliefs, and therefore may cut a larger swath than some find comfortable. If so, you may be one for whom this book can be beneficial. The goal is not consensus, as the church has no hope of ever agreeing on what the qualifications are, how to fulfill its purpose perfectly, or, for that matter, what its purpose is. The church does, however, have an obligation to be who it is and persevere in its purpose, which originally centered on recognizing and living out the church's loving connection to God, to one another, and to the rest of creation, all in the name of Jesus.

I do not take on this task lightly or write about it casually. I created an outline for this book several years ago. Occasionally I would look at it, edit it, expand it, rearrange it, and delete portions of it. As I continued to wrestle with the concepts being presented in the following chapters, I have repeatedly weighed them against my upbringing in the Roman Catholic Church, my own personal and pastoral experience, Christian history, my current Lutheran identity, long years of study (of Scripture and other sources), a deepening and evolving spiritual awareness, and a perceived understanding of the role and purpose of the church—informed both by those on the inside and those on the outside.

The diversity present among Christians and Christianity is a gift, but I won't necessarily seek audience from across that entire spectrum. Though the premises of this volume may be applicable to the entirety of the church, this book is an address primarily to the mainline church. Not because mainlines are more problematic, but the mainline church is the language and the praxis with which I'm most familiar. Others can write about the obvious need for reform within evangelical and fundamentalist traditions, but I'll leave that to them. This volume, then, will be part memoir, part theological treatise, and part plea for mainline adherents and officials, congregations, and denominations to acknowledge that we are not the church God envisions nor what the world needs. We must reclaim our core identity: the body of Christ, the community seeking to be blown by the wind of the Spirit of God, the movement launched to follow the life and teachings of Jesus of Nazareth for the sake of the world.

Even if we could ever come to some sort of agreement on the church's identity, there's still the issue of why the church exists. What is its mission? Most of us have always assumed it has something to do with "hellfire insurance," making sure we and our loved ones live eternally in heaven with God. Using my most precise theological terminology, that's a load of garbage. Simply stated, I am convinced that by following the path of Christ, the church is in existence to reveal and participate in a divine vision for the world, a more divine way of living with one another and the rest of creation. The case I'll make in this book is that this is, in fact, the default setting for all of creation, us included. This purpose can only be enacted through creative connection, love, and empathy. When the church lives out its purpose in following Christ, it will be willing to give up its own life to embrace suffering, willing to lose its self-righteous dignity to joust with the windmills of abusive power, and willing to abandon its elitist pride to recognize its home has always been its connection to the humble. If we believe anything about the life and teachings of Jesus at all, it's that our bond with Christ and the world is where hope for the world can be made real.

The assertion presented here is that the mainline church is not only best positioned to reveal this alternate reality but was created solely for that purpose. No other organization, entity, group, or clan has the capacity at its deepest core to live this out in the face of an individualized, polarized, power-seeking, and violent culture. Once again, this is our time. As weak, self-absorbed, entitled, and resistant as we are, the church was built for this very thing. All odds are stacked against it, yet the church may still show the most visible hope for the world. It took a long time for me to move beyond my own cynicism to be opened to this. I share this journey in the hope that you may be opened to it as well. And who knows after that?

There were many years when I wasn't sure there was a legitimate way for me to justify the continued existence of the church. Again and again, I witnessed a body of backward-looking, self-indulgent people who claimed the name of Christ but clamored more for power and their own justification than anything resembling the life and teachings of Jesus. I watched denominations, congregations, and ordained church leaders concerned with "sav[ing] their life" rather than "los[ing] their life for my sake, and for the sake of the gospel" (Mark 8:35). A common thread running through most of the history of the church has tied it more to corrupt systems of power and influence than to identification with the brokenness of the world. Even during the recent worldwide COVID pandemic, congregations exhibited more concern about opening their inner sanctuary doors to appease their own people than with sacrificial love for their suffering neighbors. In its concern for its own survival, the church has fallen into utilizing the same political motives

5

that have been tearing at the very fabric of the United States and other Western countries. Struggling for generational relevance, the church has successfully taught its doctrines to our youth, only to discover that the knowledge of these doctrines didn't have the effect we were hoping for. We have handed down our faith, but the faith we embraced appears incapable of carrying the current weight of our difficult and complex lives. Any attempts at reexamining our identity and purpose have only served to agitate the faithful, who have come to believe that preserving the traditions that have been passed down would somehow save us, bring young households into the fold, save the church, and turn the world around.

It seems at times that the only difference between the church and the culture in which it abides is the church's insistence on outward objects such as candles, robes, tradition, and doctrine. If the youth group has at least a few kids, we can pretend all is well. If we have a decent choir or band, can pay our bills, and gather for potlucks, we can postpone the deep examination and repentance that is necessary to be who we were created to be. No longer can the church even claim to be the sole dispenser of religious goods and services, as anyone can now be ordained a pastor on the internet for a small fee. I've been so discouraged by the similarity between the church and every other self-serving organization, government, and entity in our culture that I've been among those who have questioned the need for the church at all. Decades of work and collaboration have yielded no significant results in slowing down, much less altering, our refusal to reconsider centuries of the church's skewed emphases. Though I had considered it for several years, I finally reached a point where I felt it necessary to resign from my role as one of my own church's clergy members. A career of effort had changed virtually nothing other than my own injured mental health, depleted physical health, and inflated cynicism. I'm not arrogant enough to believe I have answers that no one else has, but all evidence reveals that the church has not done a very good job of revealing God's reign of love, peace, mercy, and compassion as taught by Jesus. A significant number of lay people, particularly the younger ones, who have given the church a chance are leaving, as they want to be part of something that can bring hope and justice into the world. For them, the church simply doesn't offer a way to do that.

A minimal amount of scratching reveals the church's resistance to looking beneath the veneer of self-justified complicity with the world around us. For me and many others, the church may have stifled itself beyond a point of no return. Short of another Holy Spirit Pentecost event more abrupt and drastic than the fire and wind described in Acts 2, there was no hope I could find. The church's existence was a waste of resources and time, and it would undoubtedly spend its dying breath defending itself and refusing to be saved. For me, that refusal signaled a depleted message of hope for the world. That may yet turn out to be true in the end, but I still don't believe the cause is completely lost.

Though the traditional Sunday school teaching about God isn't always helpful, I do, for many reasons, believe there is something divine. A more helpful personal understanding of the Divine is the subject of chapter 1, and I invite you to postpone assumptions about what I mean by "God" until reading that chapter. For now, let me say that even though I had given up on the church, Divinity apparently had not. This, despite the reality that the more divisive the church grew, the more depleted its membership became. The more trapped in memorialized ritual it stubbornly remained, the more its contemporary life and practice contrasted with its divine origin. Yet like water insistently flowing to the lowest place, the divine grace for the church kept trickling down, moistening its parched existence. It may be alright for me to let go of the superficial role to which the church had been relegated (and had relegated itself), but it showed a lack of integrity on my part to abandon what God seemed to be doing. I came to understand this in multiple ways, but I'll share one experience that profoundly caused me to rethink my plan to finally abandon the church and my role as one of its clergy.

This event involved an email from a member of a congregation where I had formerly served as pastor. This person was first exposed to the congregation through our justice work regarding the welcome, inclusion, and celebration of the LGBTQIA+ community. As a non-binary transgender person identifying as neither male nor female and more comfortable using "they/them" pronouns, this person had experienced exclusion and shame at the hands of the church, contributing to a personal belief system of rather adamant atheism. They were initially invited as an outside consultant to the congregation's "Reconciling in Christ" leadership team (a designation within my denomination specifying a congregation's openness to people of color and LGBTQ individuals) and asked to help with a congregational survey of attitudes and awareness about the queer community. Partly out of curiosity and partly as a favor to their significant other, who also served on that team, they accepted, helped, and were asked to remain on the team to continue this work of inclusion. The effect of being invited, respected, and valued had such a significant impact that when the work was completed, this atheist-now-turned-agnostic continued to have significant conversations about God, faith, and the church. Eventually, they inquired about membership in the church. They joined, and as one thing led to another, their leadership gifts became more evident. Ultimately, they were elected to a position on the church council. As the date of installing new council members approached, they discovered that they had never been baptized, a constitutional requirement for membership, much less elected leadership. This responsible council electee asked if they could remedy this and be baptized. So, a week before their installation on council, they were baptized during Sunday worship. Not the normal path, but a very joyful one, nonetheless.

Several weeks afterward, they wrote me an email explaining something that happened during their baptism. Their experience as water was poured and promises were spoken was one that brought back to them a powerful childhood vision. Whenever they recalled this image, it had always elicited calm and peace. But this time the vision was detailed, specific, and startling, occurring as the water in the baptismal font touched their forehead. In their words,

. . . Now, I've had this peaceful image my entire life, but never thought much of it, until my baptism, where it felt like the snow on my forehead. I've never experienced a physical and psychological connection like that before. The logical part of me wants to say it was the air conditioning upon my wet forehead, yet at the same time, it was such a vivid experience I cannot dismiss it. I never expected anything remotely like this to happen.

So, what does it mean? I don't know. I talked it out with my therapist, and the partial conclusion that I have drawn is that there is a lot more to God than I have given thought to. . . . I never saw God as an acting force beyond acting through what others do. Which is perhaps why the emotional part of me is uncomfortable at this manifestation. Because I think what I experienced was a connection to God. I had such a moment of introspection, I looked into the part of me that is God. If God is like a tree, and I am a fruit of the tree, during my baptism, I managed to see the branches. Now, my conflict and discomfort arises from the fact that I did no action on my part for this to happen, yet there clearly was some sort of action that happened. If it was not me, then I believe it was from God. But this means it contradicts my worldview that God is not an acting force beyond the actions of others. It is a conclusion I am not sure how to handle, and I am still struggling if it even is the right conclusion.

I was moved by the honesty and, frankly, the faith revealed within that email. The nature of the Divine goes beyond our understanding and comprehension. This former atheist, who was as unlikely to acknowledge an authentic experience of the Divine as the church was to authentically proclaim it, was willing to trust that God was connecting, that God was active, and that perhaps that was enough. It's one thing to recognize that being part of the church gave me the opportunity to hear moving stories such as this. But beyond that, although I may not be equipped or capable of advancing the divine call of the church, I can trust that perhaps I am, in some small way, part of the work that God is attempting to do through the church. And maybe that is enough.

My role has never been to save anything or anyone, but it is to do my part in what God is doing. As an unapologetic Trekkie nerd, when considering my role as a pastor in the church, I resonated with Star Trek's Seven-of-Nine as she explained to retired Admiral Jean Luc Picard her continued commitment to her futile vocation: "Ranging is my job. It's not saving the galaxy. It's helping people who have no one else to help them. It's hopeless, and pointless, and exhausting. And the only thing worse would be giving up."[3] Remaining a pastor would be my best, and perhaps my last, effort to be part of the divine work through this called, blessed, awkward, reluctant body of Christ known as the church.

Some might think this effort is fruitless and a waste of time, and I must admit, they could be right. Although I think the church as an institution has continually missed the mark, I've also occasionally seen the Divine through the work of the church, often in spite of the church itself. Somehow, I still believe there's hope for the church, but most importantly, through the church there can be a proclamation of hope for the world.

This book is an expression of that hope. If we are even willing to undertake it, the transition from the church we are comfortable with to the church we are called to be will no doubt be difficult, painful, and anxiety ridden. Though I acknowledge the chances are slim, I can't help but believe this is still the best option available for the recreation of the world in hope, love, peace, and connection—something I believe most people agree would be a good thing. In church language, that means exposing our world to the reign of God revealed in Christ.

Since this whole work about a transformed church is based on the work and default character of God, we will begin by reconsidering what we've been taught about God. The first chapter of this book delves into who or what God could be. A more accurate way to say it is that this book will begin with what *I believe* God to be. At least, what I believe today. Drawing on my very limited and elementary knowledge of theories from the world of science, particularly what physicists refer to as entanglement theory, we can

3. Frakes, dir., "Stardust City Rag," 9:42.

gain some insights about God that shed new light on the nature of the Divine. Specifically, that God, by virtue of being the creator, unifies all things in that divine image. God is the connection binding all of creation. With an expanded understanding of who God is, we may be better able to understand what God is up to. The most basic identity of a connected creation, the default setting, if you will, is this connecting nature of God.

Following that, in chapter 2 we look at the way we humans, creatures in the image of God, reveal the character of God. The unique way humanity lives out the universal truth and connectivity of God is by connecting to others in love and empathy. That is how the human portion of creation is built to reveal the image of God with the rest of creation. Compassion, empathy, and love are exclusively human ways to express our unity most fully with one another and are therefore the deepest divine expression of our humanity. Love and empathy, that divine connection to one another, is our default setting.

Chapter 3 is about Scripture. The Bible isn't an answer book that, once studied, pours some ascertainable knowledge of God into our heads. Rather, it is a description of a series of quests over multiple centuries by all kinds of people to discover something about the nature and character of God and what that looks like in their lives. We strive to know where we came from, who we are, and why we are here. Finding some universal truths sheds some light on all this. Scripture describes many who have tried, failed, and missed the mark, but also how some of these same people have nonetheless encountered, and been encountered by, the Divine. As a result of these connecting experiences, they are often moved toward expressions of more love and compassion. In discovering a connection to the Divine, they also discover they are connected to one another. In Scripture, we hear the connected image in which they were created—their default setting—reasserting itself repeatedly.

The fourth chapter deals with how we attempt to find shortcuts to this divine connection. Rather than allowing ourselves to be lowered into our core identity of love and empathy in relationship with others as a divine community, instead we try to raise ourselves up by separating ourselves from them. We mistakenly think in terms of us and them, of better and worse, of good and bad. When we emphasize existence based on these polarized dichotomies, we are attempting to come up with ways we are closer to the Divine than others. This, by definition, emphasizes not a connected community, but separation. In an effort to define ourselves, particularly against those outside the church, we have created creeds, doctrines, and catechisms, which, whether intentionally or not, too often serve to separate us from others also created in the divine image. We do so, in part, in the belief that an acceptance of these ancient documents somehow justifies us and brings us closer to God than the rest of humanity. However, instead of finding God, these sincere attempts too often serve to separate us from God as they separate us from the rest of humanity. This is an ironic counter to the connection to God that we seek.

In the next chapter, on brokenness, we can see the results of these attempts to justify and separate ourselves. Our division from each other, rather than leading us to God, leads in the opposite direction. Instead of living together in love and empathy, which is the image of God, our divisive attitudes only move us to further separation and justification. Our efforts to seek God while disconnecting from the rest of humanity (and all of creation for that matter) have significant consequences. Attempts at lifting ourselves above others can never truly bring us to God. When we continue to divisively justify ourselves in opposition to our default setting of connective love, the inevitable results can only be divisive. Racism and White supremacy, homophobia and transphobia, violence, misogyny, antisemitism, and all other types of intolerance are the result of our struggle to lift ourselves up, justifying our righteousness above others. Rather than recognizing our connection to the rest of creation, we see the Earth and its resources as mere tools to be used for our benefit. These are the manifestations of self-justification rather than divine love. If the order of creation is connection, empathy, and love, i.e., the nature of God, then nothing else can be in keeping with that natural order. Regardless of how much energy we put into that path of individuality and disconnection, it will only lead to separation and division from one another, which also leads away from the God we seek.

In chapter 6 I point out that there are always remnants outside the self-justifying, individualistic, disconnected mainstream that continue to seek divine truth, love, and compassion. These include many of the prophets of the Bible and similar voices that continue as a remnant in our era and culture. Those who speak of justice for all people together, of compassion for all regardless of circumstances, of connecting in love with the hungry and homeless, of the real threat of global climate change are the prophetic voices we can still heed. Martin Luther King Jr., Ghandhi, the Black Lives Matter movement, and the Pride celebrations of today are among those people and causes that share the prophetic role, calling us into our core identity, our default setting as people created in the divine image and therefore connected. Jesus, as the one who reveals the heart of God, is the fullest example of a remnant deliberately connecting with others who are cast off, crossing significant cultural and religious boundaries to connect in love for the sake of compassion. The church's roots were as a community in this line of prophetic remnant.

The last chapter has to do with resurrection and how the church can yet live a renewed life of hope. In the image of God, death gives way to life as the church foundationally proclaims in the resurrection of Christ. In dedicating itself to the life and teachings of Jesus, the church can emphasize priorities that are in accordance with the connective heart of the Divine. It may begin with living in relationship with those in our own congregational communities, but it cannot end there. As we recognize the significance of connected community, we bring that connectivity beyond the congregation. Connection through empathy and love for those marginalized and ignored is the default setting of the church. Rituals, doctrines, and traditions are useful if they drive us to love and empathy with an eye to those considered outsiders. However, left on their own as some sort of end unto themselves, these historic markers of church identity will lead to our continued separation, decline, and ineffectiveness; they will move us further from our divine purpose.

With some specific real-life examples, this chapter will suggest that the church, driven by the Spirit of the Divine, can yet live into its default setting, its core identity according to the connecting image of God. Which means there may just be some hope for the church's place in the world after all. No one is more surprised by this than me.

CHAPTER 1

Default

Cigars and Stardust

THE SUMMER EVENINGS IN Denver, Colorado are as idyllic as one could imagine. At a mile above sea level, the atmosphere is thin and therefore unable to hold the heat of the day. Even if the afternoon temperature tops a hundred degrees, by evening it will be in the mid-to-low seventies. The bees, active during the day, retreat to their hives before dark. It is too dry for mosquitoes. The sky is clear and the stars are bright. There isn't a more glorious place in the summertime for sitting in the quiet stillness of a backyard, sipping a wee dram, drawing on a smooth cigar, and contemplating the state of the universe.

I was engaging in this relaxing activity one evening several years ago. It was one of those rare evenings when no urgent church business hung over my head and I could indulge in a bit of mental health self-care. Totally content, I sat back and pulled on my cigar. The satisfaction was almost tangible as I watched the smoke waft away, disappearing into an infinite star-filled Colorado sky. I let my mind wander indiscriminately. It was glorious. I remember the relief of seeing my smoke disappear before it got to the next-door neighbor's house. Or did it? The aroma of a cigar can linger in the air for quite a while, and it is not everyone's favorite scent. How far would the fragrance carry in the slight breeze, even though the smoke had dissipated? Rather than being a considerate neighbor and extinguishing the cigar, I chose to sit a while longer on this perfect summer evening and ponder this dilemma. The smoke, with its alluring scent, wasn't disappearing at all. It was merely dispersing, spreading, thinning out to the point that it could no longer be seen or smelled. But of course, it was still in the air. It would always be present somehow, regardless of how far apart the smoke molecules separated and mixed with other particles that make up the atmosphere. It would become undetectable to human eyes and noses by the continuous reduction of its density, but it would still be there. I became absorbed with the thought that my little puff of cigar smoke was joining the vastness of the cosmos.

Now on a roll and continuing to risk my neighbors' goodwill, I sat and reflected. If my cigar smoke would continue to be part of the Earth's atmosphere, even in a greatly reduced form, then the rest of the atmosphere was also part of my cigar smoke. More pondering. If my grade school science teacher was correct, water evaporates into the atmosphere as vapor, condenses around particulate matter, and falls back to the earth as rain. My smoke, now part of the atmosphere, would also be part of that. This precipitation would be used in irrigation, including the growing of tobacco to make cigars. Obviously, this didn't start with my most recent puff, but had been going on for as long as cigars have been in existence. Which meant that the cigar I was enjoying at that moment had come from tobacco that had been soaked with rainfall that fell from the atmosphere that was made up of other cigar smoke, and on and on.

Cigar smoke was just the beginning that evening. Everything else that was in the atmosphere was also in the rain that watered the tobacco that became my cigar. My little puff of smoke was made from everything that was included in the atmosphere.

And why stop with the Earth's atmosphere? Everything in the known universe is made up of the same elements, including the Earth's atmosphere, the rain, tobacco crops, and my cigar. By releasing a bit of cigar smoke back into the atmosphere, I was essentially returning stardust to the universe. We are part of that universe, made up of the same elements, the same particles, just ordered a bit differently. We are unique, but we are also the same. There's a fundamental connection among all things in the universe, as all things are made of the same stuff, all interacting, all related, all joined in some vast, vague way. Later, I would read what planetary scientist and stardust expert Dr. Ashley King had to say, quoted in an article by Kerry Lotzof:

> It is totally 100% true: nearly all the elements in the human body were made in a star and many have come through several supernovas. . . . When stars die and lose their mass, all the elements that had been generated inside are swept out into space. Then the next generation of stars form from those elements, burn, and are again swept out.
>
> This constant reprocessing of everything is called galactic chemical evolution. Every element was made in a star and if you combine those elements in different ways you can make species of gas, minerals, and bigger things like asteroids, and from asteroids you can start making planets and then you start to make water and other ingredients required for life, and then, eventually, us.[1]

"That somehow seems kind of holy to me," I acknowledged to myself on that contemplative summer evening in my backyard. Contrary to real or implied Sunday school lessons, the Divine is not some old, stern, male immortal sitting high above the Earth on a heavenly throne with thunderbolts at the ready should his pent-up wrath require release. Though an admirable attempt has been made by theologians at defining God as "triune" (three persons coexisting as one God), certainly God cannot be contained by that human descriptor. Rather than a superimposed anthropomorphic entity separated from the universe, God is that which holds all things together, that which connects all things and keeps all things. God is the order of the cosmos and the cord that binds it all as one grand

1. Lotzof, "Are We Made of Stardust?," paras 1, 14–16.

creation. God is the connection; God is the unity; God is actually the gaps that we falsely believe separate us; God is the holding of all things as one, from stars to cigar smoke.

The notion of this image was compelling, and the more I considered this nature of the Divine, the less murky it appeared. I am also cognizant that whatever we call "God" is beyond our comprehension, indescribable, too vast to be understood. We owe it to ourselves to try anyway, don't we? Knowing we will get it neither fully right nor complete, we keep expanding and growing in our awareness and our experience of the Divine. If we take theology seriously as a study of universal source and truth we call God, we will seek to learn and understand as much about the Divine as possible, regardless of the source of any new understanding. With an inexpensive cigar as a catalyst, this chapter is one more attempt to broaden and deepen our understanding of, and therefore our connection to, God.

Queen of Science

Theology has an ancient history of informing, and being informed by, other disciplines. Sadly, this cooperative sharing of larger truths has waned in the last few centuries, to the particular detriment of theology. Theology, or the study of God, was designated as the "queen of science" by Thomas Aquinas somewhere around the year 1270.[2] His thinking was that theology was the first academic discipline that attempted to explain our world, how it functions, and where it came from. Soon thereafter, with the rediscovery of Aristotle's writings, the science of theology advanced and developed a helpful partnership through the Aristotelian style of thesis, antithesis, and synthesis in which each science informed the others to the advancement of all. Later, those that are now called physical sciences evolved with a more expansive view of the universe than theology had previously been able to provide. Theology and philosophy were soon relegated to the realm of soft science. Feeling

2. Oliver, "Theology," 3.

slighted, theologians pulled away from what had been a mutually beneficial relationship with other scientists and eventually were removed from the world of science completely. Theology was then replaced as the study of the universe by the physical sciences such as biology, chemistry, astronomy, and physics. Since these more tangible sciences now no longer relied on a theological worldview as their foundation, they were free to advance new discoveries and theories with imaginative directions. Theology, because its protectors refused to be informed about the universe by the new discoveries of the harder sciences, turned inward, laying sole claim to authority in an area left out of the physical sciences, that of spirituality and the afterlife. Unfortunately, many religious people today remain isolated in the prioritization of a heavenly realm rather than the continuation of a mutually beneficial relationship with the physical sciences for the purpose of discovering deeper truths. In their isolation, theologians arrogantly refused to learn anything from the advancements made by their partner scientists.

A classic and familiar example of theology exhibiting an obstinate refusal to receive new information beyond itself took place in the early seventeenth century. Galileo Galilei's support of Copernicanism rubbed everyone the wrong way because virtually all philosophers, theologians, and astronomers agreed as truth that the Earth was at the center of the universe. Each approached it differently, but each science affirmed the conclusions of the others. After 1610, when Galileo began publicly advocating a heliocentric view, which placed the sun at the center of the solar system, he met bitter opposition from pretty much every theological expert, who eventually denounced him to the Roman Inquisition early in 1615. In February 1616, the church condemned heliocentrism as "false and contrary to Scripture,"[3] and Galileo was warned to abandon his support for it, which he promised to do. When he later defended his views, he was tried by the Inquisition, found "vehemently suspect of heresy,"[4] forced to recant, and spent the rest of his life under house arrest.

3. Sharratt, *Galileo*, 127.
4. Sharratt, *Galileo*, 131.

Rather than receive this new scientific discovery, seek to understand what it added to our awareness of God, and incorporate it into an improvement of theology, religious leaders buried their heads in the sand and stood firm where they were, to the detriment of both astronomy and theology. Interestingly, no theologian today claims the Earth is the center of the universe. Thanks to undeniable scientific advances in astronomy, an awareness of God was gradually forced to include this new scientific theory.

Often kicking and screaming, theologians have been reluctant to make further advances in their understanding of God, even though some of the evidence they still denounce is rather indisputable. An obvious remnant of this fear and conceit is a refusal by some in the church to recognize the possibility of evolution, clinging for dear life to a seven-day creation mythology. Like the church authorities in 1616, evolution is deemed by some as "false and contrary to Scripture." Apparently, the conflict that many still see between religion and science has nothing to do with faith or a lack thereof. It was born out of religious fear and theological conceit.

Today, theology is considered more opinion than science. "Real" sciences deal with publicly known and agreed-upon facts. Since theology now has the reputation of dealing with myth and faerie tale, it is often disregarded by many who consider themselves intellectual. Anyone who looks to theology to help answer age-old questions of our origins and our purpose is often ridiculed, considered naïve among those who have cerebrally risen above such primitive and childish fables. Though there is some regrettable truth to this assumption, it runs counter to the true origins and purpose of the queen of science. Perhaps if theology could shake off the shackles of arrogant self-righteousness and its terror of being irrelevant, it could once again be a beneficial complement to physics rather than its opposite in the search for truth and purpose. In the meantime, that which churches continue to teach about God is founded on that seventeenth-century arrogance and ignorance rather than a deeper, collaborative search for ultimate truth. The point being that discoveries in the world of physics should again inform theology. And vice versa.

Yes, in the divine image of connection, theology has also informed physics. Because, after all, physics in some ways acknowledges faith as its starting point. Consider the explanation put forth in *The Gospel in a Pluralist Society*, by Lesslie Newbigin,[5] noted theologian, missiologist, and appreciator of science. I would highly recommend you read directly from Newbigin, as this partial explanation only pulls brief themes supporting the work of this book.

A Foundation of Faith

It's only been in the last three or four hundred years since theology and hard sciences parted ways in Western Europe. As I stated previously, that's largely due to such sciences such as astronomy, with the aid of a telescope, making discoveries about how the world works that theology refused to readily incorporate. This caused everything to come into question. If that which theology as the queen of science assumed to be true for centuries no longer held that status, then what could be trusted anymore? All the facts that experts assumed were true now had to be viewed with hard skepticism. All knowledge had to be scrutinized and reexamined. Doubt crept into every truth. Only those things that survived this new and intensive scrutiny could be retained. If it didn't pass muster, it had to be discarded. This search for absolute certainty was the only way scientific experts felt they could move from a period of dark dogmatic superstition into the light of proven truth.

The champion of this new approach of certainty was Rene Descartes, a seventeenth-century French philosopher and mathematician. His famous quote, "I think, therefore I am," served as a basis for the search for certainty of knowledge. If a hypothesis can stand up to rigorous scrutiny, doubt, and experimentation and still survive, one can be confident that it is a universal truth. It can be trusted. We can be *certain* of it. Mathematics was his prime

5. Newbigin, *Gospel in a Pluralist Society*, 27–38.

example. Mathematical laws are certain, true, and will always work. Mathematical formulas won't change but will always reveal facts in which everyone can be confident. This concept of certainty has informed science for more than three centuries now. We've been doing it so long that we have come to believe that truth can only be known through certainty. This relatively new assumption serves to further separate science from theology, which, if we're honest, cannot really be certain of much of anything.

Newbigin questioned this foundation of science by first challenging the very concept of certainty. Isn't it possible that absolute certainty is itself an illusion? To base all universal truths on the assumption that certainty is even possible requires a great leap of faith. There is no hard evidence that certainty can ever really be attained, so how can all truth rest on it? Unless, of course, one has faith that it can.

Pushing further, science can only advance when doubt, rather than certainty, is present. Doubt is what grounds a concept in reality because doubt reveals a lack of certainty. Doubt comes from a perceived gap between an unknown concept and lived experience. Even mathematical laws, which are generally assumed to surpass all doubt, are constructed from the human mind as representative of truths, and thus open to questioning. As Albert Einstein warned, "As far as the proposition of mathematics refer to reality, they are not certain; and as far as they are certain, they do not refer to reality."[6] There must be room for us to doubt that which we believe to be true, otherwise there is no connection to the reality of our everyday lives. Absolute certainty can only exist as a concept, so doubt, and therefore faith, are at the foundation of what we believe to be universal truths.

Building further on the notion of truth being understood only within reality, one only needs to consider human language. That which we believe to be truths are generally communicated through words, and words are, at best, subjective. Only through the experience of a culture where certain words have certain meanings does language have the capability of conveying an idea

6. Newbigin, *Gospel in a Pluralist Society*, 29.

or a concept. When a fact is described, there must be trust that the words used in that description will be understood by the hearer in the same way they are intended by the speaker. This notion is based on a similar cultural experience, which allows words to have assumed meaning within that culture. A simple example is the labeling of a particular four-legged creature as a "dog." With some cultural expertise, one can know what is likely meant by that term. Yet, in another culture the word "dog" may include hyenas, foxes, or wolves. When one person refers to a "dog," they are indicating a beloved family pet, while another person may be interpreting the word as a contemptible and vicious scavenger. If a level of communicative trust must be present in something as basic as labeling an animal, when there can be no absolute certainty that the term "dog" can ever be exhaustively specified, how much more faith must be present when describing what one believes to be a universal truth?

Again, for any discovery to be recognized as a scientific truth, a level of confident certainty must be attained. Once that certainty is achieved, a hypothesis can be accepted as fact, and it can be included in the pool of public knowledge. Because science, through repeated experimentation, declares with certainty that something is now a truth, everyone can be confident in believing it.

But what is it that drives the search for new truths or the expansion of currently accepted ones? More specifically, how does a scientist decide what direction to take in looking for new discoveries that may or may not reveal a scientific truth? You guessed it—faith is at the foundation. A good scientist doesn't just pick an area at random to research but comes to believe that there may be a significant discovery in a currently unknown area. As an act of faith, that scientist may devote many years of research to that project. Since a good scientist cannot afford to waste those years on research that will lead nowhere, they must truly believe the years they will spend will bear fruit and reveal a new truth or expand a current one. With no hard evidence that there is any truth to be discovered in their research, they must first believe it. And based on their faith, they may stake their reputation, even their livelihood, on the direction of this new research. Without faith, science has no direction, nowhere to begin.

Carrying this a step further, there are publicly accepted hypothetical truths that cannot be proven with any certainty. Returning to Darwin's theory of evolution, virtually all scientists believe it, yet the hard evidence leaves broad gaps that prohibit a level of certainty. Unless a better theory is put forth that can have a higher level of certainty and empirical provability, science believes this incomplete theory, often regarding it as fact. Ironically, some religious people deny the possibility of evolution for the same reason that some scientists deny the possibility of God—a lack of absolute and provable certainty. The phrase "accept it as a matter of faith" apparently depends on the topic.

The point of all this is that theology and the hard physical sciences aren't the polarities we've been taught. As described above, scientists, whether they use this language or not, are already informed by the world of faith. To be most helpful in our understanding of God and our role in creation, it is time for theologians to return to their roots and again learn from the physical sciences. This point is summarized well by Newbigin:

> If we attend only to the textbook writers and the popularizers of science, we get the impression that all this is "fact," quite different from the worlds of imagination and intuition in which poets move and from the world of faith in which religious people move. But if we look at the way scientists actually work, we see that this is a false impression. There are not two separate avenues to understanding, one marked "knowledge" and one marked "faith." There is no knowing without believing, and believing is the way to knowing.[7]

Though my undergraduate degree is in the physical science of geography, I am not a scientist by talent or desire. This chapter is by no means an attempt to explain any science to anyone. Yet it seems relevant that in discovering more about God, the world of science (including physics) does reveal some things that we

7. Newbigin, *Gospel in a Pluralist Society*, 32–33.

theologians ought to know. One theory that has proven helpful to me in attempting to grow in my understanding of the Divine is entanglement theory, which I'll attempt to describe here. Bear in mind, this isn't a physicist's description of entanglement theory, but a theologian's perspective on how an example from the world of physics can inform our understanding of God.

Entanglement

Entanglement theory was first postulated by Albert Einstein and his partners in the 1930s. Few people believed it was a real thing, including Einstein himself. Einstein was trying to describe the observed phenomenon of different molecular particles that directly affect one another, sometimes across extreme distances in space. Though there is no physical connection among them, inexplicably they are bound together in some way. Beyond simply communicating, these particles are somehow simultaneously and mutually influencing each other, as if they were one object.

When asked to explain entanglement, Dr. John Preskill, a professor of theoretical physics at Caltech, described it this way.

> It's the correlations between the parts of a system. Suppose you have a 100-page book with print on every page. If you read 10 pages, you'll know 10 percent of the contents. And if you read another 10 pages, you'll learn another 10 percent. But in a highly entangled quantum book, if you read the pages one at a time—or even 10 at a time—you'll learn almost nothing. The information isn't written on the pages. It's stored in the correlations among the pages, so you have to somehow read all of them at once.[8]

It gets even more intricate from there. According to a feature article in the fall 2019 issue of *Caltech Magazine*, entanglement theory becomes exponentially more difficult to understand when more than two particles are "entangled."

---

8. Preskill, "Quantum Entanglement," para. 2.

In natural settings such as the human body, for example, not two but hundreds of molecules or even more become entangled, as they also do in various metals and magnets, making up an interwoven community. In these many-body entangled systems, the whole is greater than the sum of its parts.

"The particles act together like a single object whose identity lies not with the individual components but in a higher plane. It becomes something larger than itself," says Spyridon (Spiros) Michalakis, outreach manager of Caltech's Institute for Quantum Information and Matter (IQIM) and a staff researcher. "Entanglement is like a thread that goes through every single one of the individual particles, telling them how to be connected to one another."[9]

Adds John Preskill, the Richard P. Feynman Professor of Theoretical Physics at Caltech, "Essentially, entanglement holds space together. It's the glue that makes the different pieces of space hook up with one another."[10]

I'm certainly not saying that an unknown connection among particles somehow proves the existence of God. Rather, I am saying that whatever our understanding of God, this unknown connection among entangled particles is an example of science informing theology as to the default setting of the universe. This entanglement theory from the world of physics reveals the same thing we see over and over in other aspects of creation: that all things are somehow connected. Like cigar smoke joining the atmosphere, this connection, this relationship among all things, is the way things are. It is the created order, the default setting, and therefore unavoidable. This aspect of physics does not just reveal the work of God, it helps us understand the very nature of God. That which entangles particles across space in some kind of mutuality is the same created order that makes all the organs of a human body function together in balance. A deep and full

9. Clavin, "Untangling," paras. 6–7.
10. Clavin, "Untangling," para. 38.

connection among all aspects of creation is, in fact, the default setting of the universe. That connection is divine.

Physicists are explaining God better than theologians in this aspect. The fact that entanglement theory is difficult to understand or explain—much less believe—doesn't seem to trouble particle physicists at all. It just means they will continue searching, experimenting, and seeking explanations. They wouldn't call it theology, but it certainly functions that way.

This doesn't mean that one must become a physicist before one can claim to know God. More to the point is that one can never claim exclusive knowledge of God merely because one claims a particular theology. There is always more to learn, always more to discover, always more to believe. As science can also teach us, we ought not repeat the isolationist mistake of seventeenth-century theologians. We must be humble enough to acknowledge what we don't know and be open to a deepening and broadening awareness of the Divine. Even if it comes from the world of science.

I don't pretend to have all this God stuff correct and neither should you. But as we share with one another across various fields of expertise, whatever we come to know about this Divinity may enable us all to grow in our understanding, and then live more fully in revealing that nature. If we believe we are created in the image of God, then living according to our default setting, or, if you prefer, according to the will of God, is the only way we can be our fullest selves. To believe we alone have knowledge of divine truth is contrary to the very truth we claim. As we will discover in the next chapter, if we seek to live as disconnected, autonomous human beings, we run counter to nature and the created order; therefore, it will never be fulfilling, life-giving, or joyous. Separating ourselves from others, whether by religion, race, sexual orientation, language, economics, or any other means, is by universal and divine definition artificial. That is the subject of the next chapter.

For Discussion

1. What is your earliest memory of God? Was it an image, a feeling, a presence, a voice? What has caused that early memory to change in your life?

2. How would you describe God now? Are there situations in your life where that view of God is inadequate?

3. How do you view the relationship between faith and science? Is there a connection for you?

4. Consider Newbiggin's statement, "There is no knowing without believing, and believing is the way to knowing." What do you think about the divinely connective idea that faith influences science as much as science influences faith?

5. Entanglement theory from the world of physics is but one scientific perspective that can help us grow in our understanding of the Divine. How can learning from a scientific worldview broaden your own awareness of God? If you consider where there are gaps in your own understanding of God, how might science be able to shed some light?

CHAPTER 2

Empathy

Fractals

LIKE A LOT OF kids of my generation, I had a collection of little Matchbox toy cars. Each boy in our neighborhood had their own assortment and, of course, their favorites. Occasionally a new Matchbox car, received as a birthday gift, would make a grand appearance on the block. This newest car would be displayed proudly by its owner and that kid immediately became the envy of the rest of us. Until someone else had a birthday, of course.

During summer vacation we would often take our tiny cars into someone's backyard and create our own miniature city. This collective endeavor could take all day as the edges of our municipality grew to the limits of the dirt pile in which we were playing. We'd use anything we could find to construct houses, office buildings, neighborhoods, parks, and, of course, roads for the cars. Available building materials would include bricks, rocks, dirt clods, leaves, an old apple, popsicle sticks, or whatever we could scrounge up.

One of the easiest parts to recreate in our miniature town would be the trees. We'd have realistic mini trees throughout our play area because any kid could just break off a small branch from a nearby tree and stick it into the ground. Viola! Instant tree, just the right size for a Matchbox metropolis. And they were amazingly faithful renditions of the full-size versions.

We were too busy trying to erect a skyscraper from a discarded shoebox to notice that our miniature trees were prime examples of the fractals commonly occurring in nature. A fractal is a pattern that is similarly repeated no matter how far you zoom in or zoom out. Our Matchbox trees, made from one small branch of a whole tree, were virtually identical patterns of that tree. The branching-out pattern from the main trunk into smaller branches is repeated along each of those branches. And repeated again on each of those smaller limbs, and again on each of those twigs. Each repetition along a branch is a smaller and smaller rendition of the same branching pattern. At the very end of each branch are tiny twigs, seemingly too small to continue the pattern. But as each twig grows into a larger branch, it too will branch off and carry on the fractal. Theoretically, into infinity.

Fractals aren't only found in Matchbox villages in some kid's backyard. They are readily seen throughout nature. Snowflakes are another prime example, as are bolts of lightning, veins of leaves, cardiovascular systems, rivers, and the details of a coastline.

Amazingly, the entirety of the universe is essentially a fractal system. The pattern of recurring connectivity that we see at a massive, universal scale we also see repeated over and over as we move to smaller and smaller scales, all the way down to the tiniest microscopic level. The fractal connection of creation that can be seen in the expanse of galaxies, solar systems, and ecosystems is basically duplicated in a single cell or molecule.

It then makes sense that each individual human being would also be a fractal representation of the image of God in which we are created. Since the essential nature of God is connection, it would follow that this default setting would be repeated in all that God has made. Each person is part of this divine fingerprint, a fractal pattern of mutual interconnectivity. We are part of an infinite fractal pattern that repeats the nature of God over and over. Rather than repeating branch patterns of a tree or continuing crystal patterns of a snowflake, we see recurring patterns of interconnected compassion, mutuality, and reciprocation in each of us. If the divine image is interconnection, a smaller fractal of that is revealed in human physiology. You don't have to look very far to see the repeating pattern of divine connectivity over and over within and among us. We are fractals. This is true.

Biology

Take, for example, human physiology. As a refresher in what most of us have forgotten from biology class, each human body has ten different functioning systems, each made up of multiple parts that work together to serve a particular purpose. For example, a person's circulatory system is made up of sixty thousand miles of blood vessels, with the heart pumping blood constantly through every part of this very complex network. The blood pumped through the circulatory system picks up life-giving oxygen that has been inhaled by the lungs. The circulatory system delivers that oxygen to all the cells of the body and picks up any waste created by these cells to deliver it to the kidneys and lungs for disposal.

Though each system within the body is an entirely separate system, they are all connected in a mutually dependent way for them to work. It doesn't do the body any good to pump blood if it can't pick up oxygen from the respiratory system. In the same way, the whole body would fail if the digestive system wasn't able to make nutrients available for the circulatory system to deliver to all the bodily organs.

Even seemingly unrelated body systems are connected. The skeletal system relies on the urinary system to remove waste produced by bone cells; in return, the bones of the skeleton create a secure structure that protects the bladder and other urinary system organs. The circulatory system delivers oxygen-rich blood to your bones to keep them alive. Reciprocally, the bones are busy making new blood cells.[1]

1. Live Better Team, "You Can't Have One," 1.

Every system, organ, tissue, and cell in each human body is dependent on all the other systems connecting and working together for the sake of the whole body. If one fails, all will fail. This is the way each human body is built to work. Without exaggeration, it is safe to say that connectivity is how each one of us stays alive. This mutual reciprocity in each human body is a fractal of the connective image of God.

The apostle Paul has some understanding of this and uses it when he writes of the church as "being baptized into one body" (1 Corinthians 12:13). He refers to all parts of the church being mutually dependent on one another. Though separate, they function in an interconnected way, just like the various parts of a human body.

> As it is, there are many members, yet one body. The eye cannot say to the hand, "I have no need of you," nor again the head to the feet, "I have no need of you." On the contrary, the members of the body that seem to be weaker are indispensable, and those members of the body that we think less honorable we clothe with greater honor, and our less respectable members are treated with greater respect. (1 Corinthians 12:20–23)

If biology can help us understand more about our own physical nature as human beings, it also can help us understand more about how we each reflect the nature of the Divine. The characteristic of God emphasized in the previous chapter is that by default the nature of God is connection. If we trust somehow that we are created in the image of God, then we are created in the divine image of connection. As human biology and physiology reveal, interconnectedness is our default setting.

Beyond Biology

This interconnection goes beyond human physiology. The entirety of who we understand ourselves to be, all aspects that comprise our identity, intertwine and inform each other.

There was a period in my life when I was confronted with depression. An unusual set of experiential circumstances brought on such stress that it affected the totality of who I am. Depression isn't merely feeling melancholy or tiredness. It isn't a weakness or giving in to sadness. It's not selfish or feeling sorry for oneself. Depression is a physical manifestation brought on by bio-chemical changes in the brain. It involves a physiological malfunction of the body's serotonin receptors, situated in the hypothalamus, which link the nervous system to the endocrine system. Like many other diseases, there are treatments for depression—both medicinal and therapeutic.

Fortunately, I had access to and received both remedies. This treatment involved caring for multiple aspects of who I am as a human: emotional, mental, and physical. These were all interwoven and were affected by a disease brought on from a set of external conditions in my life. One lasting result of this whole experience is that I am more acutely aware of the interconnection among all aspects of who I am. My physical body was affected by one relatively small chemical imbalance in my brain, but my emotions and even my thought processes functioned differently too. Every part of me that makes me the person I am was affected in profound ways by this chemical difference. Whether obvious or not, whether it made sense or not, whether I accepted it or not, all of me was connected and functioning together. In truth, all aspects of who I am are interwoven, reciprocal, and interdependent. Connection is my default setting.

Accepting that reality is key to understanding how we are designed to function as individuals, as communities, and societies. As a fractal system, our individual selves reveal the same connecting pattern as the universe. That same pattern can readily be seen when we look at relationships, human communities, and societies. By nature, we work best when we live into our default setting of mutual connection, whether we like it or not. The problem is that we usually don't like it.

The Barrier of Autonomy

Mutual connectivity is the default fractal setting from the vastness of the cosmos to individual particles, from each person's body systems to their mental and emotional functioning. It follows, then, that connection is also the core nature of every human community, of every culture as a whole. Though contrary to our created nature, most of us desire to function autonomously without depending on others within our community. Despite our noble attempts, it just cannot be done. At least not in a way that we can truly thrive. Autonomy is often longed for, yet it defies the default setting of us as individuals, the universe, the very nature of the Divine. This autonomous perspective can readily be seen in political policies toward the poor, e.g., "pull yourself up by your own bootstraps," and in power struggles meant to convey one person's wealth and existence as vastly more important than that of an impoverished or unhoused individual. An unnatural desire for autonomy is evidenced even within the culture of the Western church itself.

Underlying many of our good Christian intentions and acts of unselfish service is the assumption of autonomy. We aren't even aware of it, and yet we nonetheless assume the reality of this counter-narrative. In doing so, the church generally opposes its very nature, its default setting of divine connection, interdependence, and mutuality.

The members of most congregations believe they exist primarily to serve others. That is a goal to be attained, and a lofty value that is commendable and virtuous. We organize congregations around this understanding, establish practices to enhance this understanding, and speak openly about the ways in which we serve our communities. We make serving part of our mission statements. We put it on banners. We utilize it as a theme for our conferences and assemblies. Serving the world is often at the heart of our missional self-understanding. Our interpretation of Scripture justifies this starting point. We no longer question the truth of the assumption that we are here to serve. We speak of Jesus entering the world to serve the world, even to the point of dying for it. Congregations, in turn, understand their role—their identity—in a similar fashion. We exist to serve the world, and in so doing hope to reveal Christ through our service. Does this sound about right so far?

The common agreement that the church is here to serve is often the starting point when a church develops relationships with individuals, other congregations, or other organizations in the broader community. They ask, who in the community needs help, who is hurting, who needs to be served? The answers to these questions are largely the basis for launching into relationships—relationships that allow congregations to serve. They seek out the poor, the hungry, the homeless, and the disadvantaged. They support, supply, and partner with agencies and institutions in their communities that share their concern for the needy people in their neighborhoods. They do what they need to do to serve those who need their help.

How can anyone find fault with that? How can this accepted truth come into question? As sincere and good as this orientation of service is, it can sometimes counter the default setting of the universe and the nature of God. Depending on our awareness and how we approach it, beginning with the assumed truth that primarily we are "here to serve" often assumes that we first need to gather the resources necessary to serve. If we are to serve the poor, we believe that we must have enough financial resources to give money away. If we are to serve the hungry, we first must have excess food to share. If we are to serve the spiritually searching, we first have to spend time putting our theological ducks in a row. Consistent with and informed by an American culture that supposes autonomy as a strength, the starting point of serving for many congregations is the acquisition of resources. We feel a need to make sure there is at least enough to sustain ourselves and only then consider those we seek to serve. Basically, once we believe we have enough for ourselves (generally with much disagreement over how much is enough), we dole out the leftovers in acts of charity. This can explain why so many congregations are now giving less to their governing bodies. In the midst of a global pandemic, the fear of not having enough for ourselves increased. This, in turn, led to a proportionate increase in a felt need for autonomy.

Rather than interconnection or reciprocity, serving from a position of autonomy comes from a position of power. We believe that charity receivers need us in the church because we have acquired what they need. Serving can often imply that the connection a congregation has with recipients of benevolence is a one-way street. You are dependent on us but we can get along fine without you. If service only goes one way, that severely limits the divine connection between the server and those served.

This starting place of autonomous serving is largely accepted as truth, but have you thought about how restricting that can be? The connecting nature of God, as the mutuality among the three divine persons in the doctrine of a triune God attempts to reveal, is not defined in service only, but through genuine connections where congregations both serve and are served. If we aren't careful, we may discover that "we are here to serve" may rest on a foundation of striving for the power innate in autonomy. We may unconsciously assume that in order to serve others, we cannot need anyone or anything. This is the opposite of the nature of God, and therefore must also be the opposite of the identity of the church.

Jesus models an interconnected *autonomy-not* within his culture by both serving and being served. Anthony Gittins points this out: "For Jesus, the solution to the problem of hierarchy and dominance was to be both master and servant, both one up and one down, both host and guest, both stranger and host."[2] Several biblical stories reveal Jesus as welcoming, requesting—even needing—service from those around him. The woman who anointed Jesus with the expensive ointment of pure nard (Mark 14:3–9), the boy who offers his lunch of fish and bread (Matthew 14:15–21), the Samaritan woman at the well who gives a thirsty Jesus a drink of water (John 4:1–26), and Jesus' passionate request that his three closest disciples stay awake with him during his most difficult hour at Gethsemane (Matthew 26:36-45) exemplify this. Jesus was not

2. Gittins, *Ministry at the Margins*, 147.

autonomous but approached ministry from the perspective of relationship and sharing resources. Jesus was connected to those around him in a manner revealing the divine nature.

Later in this book we'll look at how when we struggle to avoid the default connective setting, we miss the mark. Anything other than divine connection to God and to others ends up posing problems. The good news is that connection is our default setting, so it's honestly a matter of removing the additional layers we've superimposed and being who we are designed to be. But we'll get to that later. Right now, let's consider how we humans do connect to one another. Again, this is natural, our default setting, and is what it means to be fully human and a fully human society.

Empathy

Each individual human being is made up of a set of connective systems, processes, chemicals, organs, and emotions. These cooperative, mutually interdependent connections allow each one of us to survive. Yet the fractal model at the beginning of this chapter states that connecting isn't limited to any one facet of the created order. Rather, connection is the default setting of every portion of creation. It is, theologically speaking, the image of God.

The connections that humans experience can be seen within the systems of each individual person, but also among other people in a community. As a natural fractal of the connected created order, we are designed to connect with one another in community. When one person experiences a mutual connection with another person, we refer to that as empathy.

> [Empathy is] the ability to recognize, understand, and share the thoughts and feelings of another person, animal, or fictional character. Developing empathy is crucial for establishing relationships and behaving compassionately. It involves experiencing another person's point of view, rather than just one's own, and

enables prosocial or helping behaviors that come from within, rather than being forced.[3]

Though apparently not unique to humans (some studies show that other primates, dogs, and even rats can exhibit basic forms of empathy),[4] we humans experience empathy at a deeper and more profound level. It plays a necessary role in the way we develop and maintain relationships and even how we experience the social structure of family.

Empathy is hardwired into our brains, perhaps even into our bodies. Reflecting the divine image of interconnectivity, we humans are created to connect with one another at a significant level. Part of being fully human is understanding what another person is feeling and experiencing. The deeper the relationship, the more connection involved. Empathy and love are the default setting of our created order as humans.

Empathy is truly a human expression of the Divine. The image of God in which we are created is naturally experienced through our empathy, love, and compassion toward others. These are the human traits that connect us to one another. They are the particularly human ways of exhibiting the same connection that makes up the entire universe. The default setting for humans is to connect, to be in relationship, to love, to empathize. Theologically, the wider the circle of empathy, the more we are taking part in God's will for us. This is living in the reign of God that Jesus talked about. The deeper the *imago Dei,* the further the reaches of those connections.

The opposite of connection through empathy is disconnection through isolation, individualism, and autonomy. At its extreme, people who are diagnosed as psychopaths or sociopaths are unable to empathically connect with others, living their lives emotionally separated from anyone else. Unable to connect with another person's thoughts, feelings, or experiences, this lack of empathy can allow those afflicted to cause great harm to others.

3. "Empathy," para. 1.
4. Ekman, "What Is Empathy?," para. 3.

As we'll discover in a later chapter, a deliberate avoidance of connection, a withdrawal of empathy, is responsible for virtually all of humanity's woes.

Gospel writer Matthew records Jesus speaking of empathy as a major tenet of the Jewish faith when he writes, "In everything do to others as you would have them do to you; for this is the law and the prophets" (Matthew 7:12). This basic ability to consider how your actions affect the lives of others has been referred to as the "Golden Rule" and is a standard lesson starting in childhood. This is basic empathy; it is connection; it is an awareness that we cannot live separately, apart from others. It is our social default setting. It is being fully human. It is the image of God.

For Discussion

1. Fractals are repeating patterns that can be potentially duplicated from a cosmic level all the way down to a microscopic view. How might fractals inform the theological stance that human beings are created in the image of God?

2. A major theme in this chapter is that the nature of God is interconnectivity and is, therefore, foundational to all life. If all aspects of an individual's full identity work in connection together and reveal a divine nature, what does that say about such difficult connections as severe anxiety manifesting in physical illness? Is that the image of God? Why or why not?

3. Despite reciprocity and mutuality being the nature of creation, humans often desire to live autonomously—individually, communally, and corporately. If that is in opposition to the image of God, why do you think we devote so much time and energy to achieve it? Can you see any harm in working toward autonomy?

4. Empathy is a deep way human beings connect to one another. As such, it reveals the image of the Divine. In which areas of your life do you struggle to be empathetic, e.g., business, politics, finances, theology? Why do you think you choose to

separate yourself from others in these arenas? How can you begin to be more open to validate others' views and experiences according to the divine image?

CHAPTER 3

Truth

Scripture, Dammit

SEVERAL YEARS AGO, MY denomination was still struggling with whether LGBTQIA+ people in same-sex relationships could officially be ordained as pastors and deacons and included on our clergy roster. Additionally, the church was trying to decide whether long-term, monogamous, same-sex relationships could be "blessed." Many meetings were held, studies sponsored, and positions taken. Although numerous people sincerely intended to listen to the stories and struggles of queer Christians and the fears of many straight, cisgender Christians, the vast majority simply dug their heels in, clinging to previously held positions on the matter. Few minds were changed, and few prejudices overcome. Rather than seeking to understand or grow in awareness, people chose instead to justify their positions using some kind of higher authority as evidence of the truthfulness of their position. In the church the highest authority available was the Bible. It was referred to often during these proceedings, with amazingly different interpretations, depending on the position on gay ordination taken by a given individual.

At one gathering of my regional judicatory where this topic was high and hot on the agenda, microphones on the floor were opened for participants to state their cases. Lines immediately formed and grew longer as passionate people tried to put forth their insightful biblical perspective. Those lined up to share their scriptural wisdom soon became divided into two main camps: those in favor of allowing LGBTQ people to be ordained and those opposed. The lines became so long that if everyone lined up at the microphones was allowed to speak, the meeting would have dragged on for hours, or even days, longer than scheduled. Further, after an extended amount of time, it became clear that the arguments being presented were becoming repetitive. The presider observed that all points of view had apparently been shared and therefore only a few more people would be allowed to speak on this issue. Most people had grown weary by this time and the sense of relief was palpable.

I remember a particular woman who had only recently stepped up to the speakers' line. When she saw that she wouldn't get to say her piece, she dejectedly returned to her seat, muttering, "But I had Scripture, dammit." I have no doubt that she did. Although her interpretation may have been the one that would have opened minds and hearts in new and wondrous ways, I sincerely had my misgivings. We tend to use the Bible to bolster our own perspectives rather than be shepherded into deeper truths. Ironically, interpretation of the Bible often appears to be at the heart of Christian division.

Journal

For most Christians, the Bible is spoken of as a sacred book depicting the truth about God, the world, the church, and us. We call it inspired, authoritative, and revelatory. We claim it to be God's written word among us. Some even go so far as to consider the Bible inerrant and infallible, selecting particular verses and interpreting them in a literal sense to proclaim God's ultimate truth for all people in all times and in all places. Clearly important to most Christians, the Bible is also a source of controversy, which then, obviously, becomes an issue.

Many Christians have transferred their need for certainty (as described in chapter 1) from science to Scripture. There are some who would suggest that our quest for ultimate and certain truth cannot include science because scientists begin at a different place. The argument says that scientists generally aren't concerned with proving the existence of God, so their search for truth doesn't begin from a foundation of the Divine. On the other hand, the Bible, we have been told, assures us that God is truth. If so, this reasoning states, Scripture demands that the search for ultimate truth must begin with a belief in God. Because the sacred Scriptures presume the existence of God, these writings can reveal a deeper truth about God than physics or biology ever could. God is truth and the Bible reveals God's truth; therefore truth can only be found in the Bible. This circular argument provides the certainty many seem to desire, shallow as it may be.

The fear and arrogance that sixteenth-century theologians displayed to discount the scientific theory of heliocentricity lives on in this search for certainty through the Bible. It results in a distorted, naïve, and supercilious understanding of God, and therefore of the church. Rather than taking an honest risk of seeking deeper truth and larger awareness of the Divine, we misuse Scripture to justify our pre-existing personal belief system. Sometimes these beliefs are supported by a particular church culture and sometimes they are shaped by that church culture. Regardless, whenever we are certain that we alone have knowledge of ultimate truth, we are in dangerous—and ungodly—territory.

Instead of thinking of the Bible as the book containing all deific knowledge and factual answers, it may be more helpful to understand it as a collection of writings depicting many people's historic search for, discovery of, and connection to the Divine. We are fortunate to have many centuries' worth of pondering, attempting, experimenting, sharing, and theorizing about what God and God's purpose for the world might be. Much of biblical writing comes from some of the wisest, most prayerful, and most genuinely sincere seekers of God. And some of it comes from—well, to be kind—others. The Bible isn't an individual answer book, but a mutual journal of connective discovery. As one moves through Scripture, it is relatively easy to see a progression in the expansion of belief and awareness of God. From a worldview of a flat Earth covered in a dome all the way to the promise of a new kingdom of justice, the Bible reveals a journey of encounters and new understandings of the presence and nature of God.

Bias

Anyone who reads Scripture already has a bias in its interpretation. Just the fact that you read it begs the question regarding personal preference. I'm guessing if you have read the Bible at all, you've read it in English. And if you are reading this book now, you weren't alive when any portion of the Bible was first written. Since not one word of the Bible was originally written in English (not even King James English), it has been translated from other languages into a language we can understand. In fact, none of the original documents of Scripture exist (that we know of), so what we have at best are copies of copies. And since none of us were alive in Palestine two thousand years ago, our contemporary worldview isn't sufficient to translate directly across multiple centuries and cultures.

Regardless of what we may believe about the process involved in making the Bible understandable in some form, it has already been interpreted by some scholar (or a team of scholars) who have their own biases. Was God at work, moving all those people to be as accurate as possible? Of course. For many of them, this was their entire life's work, and they prayerfully and devotedly took great pains to present biblical pages that were precise and reliable. Biased, but reliable as far as they were concerned. Were they inspired? No doubt whatsoever. But we would then have to come to agreement on our various interpretations of "inspired."

This isn't a knock on the Bible's accuracy or reliability. Quite the contrary. The fact that the verses of Scripture connect so many people to a stronger faith and motivate so many people to imitate Christ is nothing short of amazing. Especially considering the biases we each bring to its interpretation.

You may prefer the New Revised Standard Version in American English over the Jerusalem Bible, for instance. Or you might find *The Message* to be more enlightening than the New International Version. Before you can begin to defend your own interpretation of Scripture over someone else's, you need to be honest about the biases that lead you to have those preferences. By definition, we who have grown up in a twenty-first-century Western culture see the world differently than first-century Jewish Palestinians. We all have assumptions and biases, and until we acknowledge them openly and truthfully, it is difficult to grow in our understanding of what the Bible contains. Chances are, each of us holds biases that favor our currently held belief system. We read into Scripture that which we already perceive to be true, thus justifying our current opinions and values. That, unfortunately, becomes a major barrier to seeking larger truths that may broaden and deepen what we believe about the Divine and our connection therein.

More than just the language and the version of Scripture we read, our biases affect how we interpret Scripture itself. If we believe the Bible to be without error from the table of contents to the maps, that may reveal a personal bias regarding a previously asserted need for certainty, which affects how we interpret its passages. Contrast that with a perspective provided by the Rev. Dr. Rachael Powell, who wrote that the Bible, "from Genesis to Revelation, has one dominant narrative: The pervasive action of God, throughout Scripture, is to create life and to bring individuals and peoples through death to resurrection."[1] That leads to significantly different and, in my experience, deeper interpretations. Who's right? Who has the truth? Who has the correct interpretation? As I've heard it said, "If I know I'm right, I don't have to listen to anyone else."

The point here is that biases exist in each of us. Therefore, it is important that we recognize them and how they affect our view

1. Powell, *God's People Made New*, 39.

of Scripture and our interpretation of it. Without taking that step, we are limiting our ability to recognize a connection to God and to the wisdom and inspiration that meet us in the Bible.

Facts

Contrary to a long-standing personal policy, I recently became involved in a theological debate with an acquaintance on a major social media platform (don't judge me). The topic isn't relevant, but my debating partner was insisting that their stance on the issue was the correct one, because it's clear in the Bible. They proceeded to quote some verses to show me the plain evidence right there in black and white. Rather than argue about context, history, literary style, or differences in culture and time, I attempted to point out that their interpretation was but one way to read those verses. In my own faithfulness, I happened to interpret them quite differently. I believed my friend's perspective was consistent with their faith and values and told them so. Mine was consistent with my own as well. The basis on which we each interpreted those verses was the difference. Alas, my social media companion got the last word. "I see. You do not believe the words actually mean what they mean." I abandoned the conversation, deeply saddened that according to my friend, my interpretation of Scripture, based on many decades of searching, studying, verifying, listening, testing, and, yes, debating, was simply invalid because I didn't consider the words of Scripture to be absolutely, plainly factual. At least not in the way that they did. In their mind, only one of us could have the correct interpretation. No surprise that my debate partner was certain that the correct interpretation was theirs.[2] For them, the words of the Bible provide facts. Facts allow for certainty. Certainty equals truth. Argument settled.

There are two major problems with this line of thinking. One is the fallacy of certainty as described in the first chapter of this book (you may want to refer again to the subsection "A

2. To be fair, I also believed my interpretation of those verses was more correct and more faithful.

Foundation of Faith" in chapter 1). The other is the whole issue of "facts." Our cultural reliance on accurate facts as the revealer of truth is a very recent development. The whole notion of trusting in provable facts, and only those facts, came about during the Enlightenment period of the eighteenth century. Again, it was during this time that science and theology were parting ways. Prior to the Enlightenment, religious folk, and everyone else for that matter, considered truth to be anything that consistently held together over time and was also in keeping with what was already known. In other words, consistency and tradition were the criteria for truth. Dr. David Lose explains, "For the most part, [in the pre-Enlightenment world] there were two main criteria for something to be considered true. First, it had to be logically consistent. You know, your argument had to hold together . . . [Second], fidelity to tradition. In essence, what you say is true can't contradict what people have known is true for centuries."[3]

After the Enlightenment, however, the tradition aspect began to give way to verifiability. Rather than trusting as truth that which was tried and true, accepted truth now shifted toward those things that could be proven. Consistency and facts became the emerging criteria for truth. This new way of filtering truth has become so deeply engrained that we cannot imagine any other way of doing it. Which is unfortunate when we look at the truth of Scripture. If we limit ourselves to our contemporary, post-Enlightenment, Western cultural view of truth, we end up imposing a set of conditions about truth that were unknown until two or three centuries ago. Lose describes it like this:

> We live in a post-Enlightenment world where rational proof is highly valued. And so it feels like it would be a little easier if we could prove things in the Bible like we can prove how the light bulb works. Which might be why so many people treat the Bible like a divine reference book, reading it like it's a book of facts instead of a book of faith.[4]

3. Lose, *Making Sense of Scripture*, 41.
4. Lose, *Making Sense of Scripture*, 46.

Obviously, all authors of Scripture wrote their portion of the Bible before the Enlightenment. Therefore, they couldn't operate from our rational proof worldview. They weren't writing to convey facts as we know them. They were writing to express deeper, more substantial truths. Even if they could understand our twenty-first-century Western perspective of truth, verifiable facts didn't really occur to them as important.

Take, for example, the book of Matthew. The author of this Gospel wrote somewhere around 70–90 CE, about a half century after the death of Jesus. His audience was largely Jewish, probably living in or near Antioch of Syria, and had only recently experienced the destruction of the temple in Jerusalem (70 CE) and the first Jewish-Roman War (66–73 CE). That community was largely comprised of Jewish believers in Jesus who were struggling to figure out what faith in this Messiah meant during all the violence and destruction around them. The author rarely had to explain Jewish customs, traditions, and laws because, as Jews, his audience was already intimately familiar with them. To help them make sense of what was meant for Jesus to be the Messiah, Matthew used the basic story of Mark's Gospel, along with another unknown source (also used by Luke) generally referred to imaginatively as Q, or Quelle (German for "source"). Matthew[5] added his own particular emphasis to convey the most important thing for him—a truth, if you will—that Jesus of Nazareth, crucified and risen, was the Messiah promised by God to their ancestors. The author includes as "proof" many prophecies from Hebrew Scripture that he asserts were fulfilled by Jesus. Multiple times he compares Jesus to Moses through story, analogy, and verbiage, likening him to this great hero of the Jews. Moses was the one chosen by God to lead the Hebrew people out of slavery and through the wilderness to the promised land—the primary story of Hebrew Scripture. Are all the incidents and fulfillments Matthew depicts verifiably factual? For him, that wasn't what made his telling of Jesus-as-the-Messiah true. Consider a brief section of Matthew as a case in point.

---

5. "Matthew" likely wasn't the author's real name—so much for the Bible reporting only facts.

Commonly referred to as "The Slaughter of the Innocents," Matthew 2:13–23 describes Joseph, Mary, and the child Jesus fleeing for their lives from the wrath of the unscrupulous King Herod, who upon hearing the magi describe this newborn child as the "king of the Jews" believed Jesus to be a threat to his power. They took refuge in Egypt until Herod died.

> Now after [the wise men] had left, an angel of the Lord appeared to Joseph in a dream and said, "Get up, take the child and his mother, and flee to Egypt, and remain there until I tell you, for Herod is about to search for the child, to destroy him." Then Joseph got up, took the child and his mother by night, and went to Egypt and remained there until the death of Herod. This was to fulfill what had been spoken by the Lord through the prophet, "Out of Egypt I have called my son."
>
> When Herod saw that he had been tricked by the magi, he was infuriated, and he sent and killed all the children in and around Bethlehem who were two years old or under, according to the time that he had learned from the magi. Then what had been spoken through the prophet Jeremiah was fulfilled: "A voice was heard in Ramah, wailing and loud lamentation, Rachel weeping for her children; she refused to be consoled, because they are no more."
>
> When Herod died, an angel of the Lord suddenly appeared in a dream to Joseph in Egypt and said, "Get up, take the child and his mother, and go to the land of Israel, for those who were seeking the child's life are dead." Then Joseph got up, took the child and his mother, and went to the land of Israel. But when he heard that Archelaus was ruling Judea in place of his father Herod, he was afraid to go there. And after being warned in a dream, he went away to the district of Galilee. There he made his home in a town called Nazareth, so that what had been spoken through the prophets might be fulfilled, "He will be called a Nazarene."

Three times in this short narrative Matthew refers to the words of prophets being fulfilled. In describing this horrendous event in the early life of Jesus, additional and obvious references are made to the common Old Testament modes of God speaking through dreams, prophecies proclaimed, and (akin to Moses) even utilizing Egypt as a place God sends God's chosen ones. This sounds good to everyone, including us, who hear it with twenty-first-century ears. The only problem for fact-as-truth-based folks is that this event never happened. There is no reliable historical record anywhere of Herod making such a history-making decree, much less carrying it out. Killing all children in Bethlehem under the age of two would surely have been referenced by someone other than Matthew somewhere. Not even any of the other Gospel writers mention this event. Matthew was quite aware of that fact, but that wasn't his point. Was Matthew lying? Not at all. Herod was widely documented as a cruel tyrant who ruthlessly killed a lot of people. Matthew's audience could certainly relate to those legends and stories about him. This narrative keeps with the accepted tradition of Herod (meeting both pre-Enlightenment factors necessary for truth: tradition and consistency) but serves a deeper, more truthful purpose. In fleeing to Egypt and later returning to live in Nazareth, Jesus fulfills three prophecies from Hebrew Scripture. It is only God's Messiah who does that, so the fulfillment of what was written by the prophets is the truth Matthew seeks to convey. Historical fact? Not likely. True? Absolutely.

Throughout the Bible there are countless examples of this same perspective of truth. It's unfair and unfaithful to limit the truth of Scripture to our very recently developed notion of how something is true. There's so much more going on. Again, David Lose sums it up:

> If the Bible is mainly a divine reference book, then the biblical writers are mostly sharing facts with us. But if they're confessing things they think are true but can't prove, then there's an urgency about it. They're not just worried about getting the facts right. Rather, they want to persuade us of this really huge, but at times hard to believe, truth that might just change our lives if we believe it.[6]

6. Lose, *Making Sense of Scripture*, 53.

Truth

All that said, Christians throughout the world take the authority of Scripture seriously. A question we must ask is why? Why is the Bible held as trustworthy and as a source of truth for so many? This reflects back on how we understand truth. Again, if the prerequisite of truth is verifiable facts, then the authority of Scripture must rest on believing that the events described in the Bible are factual history. If there is a threat to the historic validity of any part of Scripture, the entirety of it would become unreliable. I've heard it said like this: "If you can't trust the truth of a six-day creation as described in Genesis 1, how can you trust the truth of the resurrection of Jesus?" If any part of the Bible can be "proven" as "untrue," then its authority as a book of truth crumbles.

That's a lot of pressure. When that need for certainty, nested in our new post-Enlightenment concept of truth, is threatened, we can make some rather bizarre stretches in our Bible reading. For example, the science of geology verifiably proves the Earth is 4.5 billion years old, which threatens such things as the historical accuracy of the recorded ancestry of Jesus. In the Gospel of Luke this is laid out all the way back to Adam, the first human, son of God (Luke 3:23–38). Luke lists a line of seventy-six ancestors, each of which is recorded as the son of a named father. Since Genesis says that Adam was created on the sixth day of the brand-new world's existence (Genesis 1:26–31), that would mean that each parent would have to have been, on average, almost sixty million years old when the next generation was born. If, that is, geologists are correct. I've read through the Bible a time or two, and I can't recall a single instance where someone is recorded in the Bible as becoming a parent at the ripe old age of sixty million. When looking at this genealogy in Luke, the only other option available to the Bible-as-facts crowd is that geologists must be wrong; the Earth simply cannot be that old. And that's that.

However, using the concept of truth more likely understood by the writer of Luke's Gospel, it's possible that through this genealogy the author is more concerned about making a parallel between Jesus and Adam. Whereas Adam failed in his attempt to resist temptation in the garden of Eden,[7] Jesus was success-ful in accomplishing that feat in the wilderness (Luke 4:1–13). Which, not coincidentally, are the verses immediately following Jesus' ancestral line. Adam, the first son of God, was defeated by the devilish snake. But Jesus, Son of God and the new Adam, overcame the devil. That seems like a truth that most Christians could grab hold of. That is, once we let go of our need for biblical certainty through provable, historical facts.

Authority

We can certainly say that the Bible is true, or at least contains truth, even though the history described may be a bit factually suspect in places. That doesn't account for the Bible's recognized authority by most people in the church. What makes the Bible authoritative? Or, backing up, is the Bible really authoritative?

For something or someone to have any kind of authority, that authority must be given. Authority is granted when the holder of that authority is trusted as authoritative. If this sounds like a circu-lar argument, that's probably because it is. The short answer is that the Bible is authoritative to Christians because Christians trust it is authoritative, and therefore give it that status.

Muslims don't consider the Bible as authoritative as Chris-tians do, because for them it isn't trusted as authoritative. The Quran, however, is a recognized authority within Islam. Jews grant authoritative status to the Torah, law, and prophets, but don't give authority to the Christian New Testament. Even within Christian-ity itself, the apocryphal intertestamental books are authoritative within the Roman Catholic and Eastern Orthodox traditions while often virtually disregarded by most other Christians.

Beyond religious scriptural writings, the authority of gov-ernments, officeholders, law enforcement, and more has been given by those who trust them as authoritative. There are times

7. It's really a pretty good story. Check it out in the third chapter of Genesis.

when a person or an entity loses a level of trust, and their authority is revoked and given to another. Those involved in the Black Lives Matter movement were attempting to make this point. In part, the argument is that the institution of local police can't be trusted to dispense justice fairly, resulting in a higher percentage of Blacks than Whites being arrested, abused, imprisoned, and even killed for similar offenses (or non-offenses). Black Americans have been saying that the police can't be trusted with the authority they enjoy; therefore that authority needs to be reconsidered and placed with a more representative, less violent entity that all can trust, especially African Americans, who, if you want to talk about verifiable historical facts, have been on the short end of the justice stick in this land since 1619.

Authority is a recognized commodity that is given because trust in that authority is widely accepted. The difficulty comes when different people or entities are trusted by different groups of people. Authority only works when those subject to that authority can trust that authority.

The ancient people of Israel recognized as authoritative certain people at certain times who spoke to God for them and to them on God's behalf. These "judges" came to be trusted as long as people continued to experience them as leaders of faithfulness and justice. As trust in a particular judge grew, that one was eventually seen as authoritative and was given agency to rule on behalf of the people. If they continued to be trusted, a judge remained in a position of authority. Samuel, for instance, was recognized as a judge of Israel when they were being threatened by the terrifying Philistines. According to the book of 1 Samuel, chapters 7–8, Samuel had been coaxing the Israelites to pray, repent, and follow God's ways for some time, and that was beginning to take hold. When the Philistines began to approach Israel in their typically fearsome way, the people of Israel ran to Samuel, pleading with him to pray that they would be saved from their enemy. Samuel did, and they were. The Israelites overcame the Philistines and there was peace between them.

If Samuel could ask God to intervene against the mighty Philistines and God did it, apparently Samuel could be trusted, and authority was given to him as a judge for the rest of his life. Almost.

As Samuel got older, he began to delegate some of his judging responsibilities to his children. They hadn't earned genuine trust from the Israelites and weren't respected as authoritative figures. As a result, the people began to lose trust in Samuel too. After all, he was making some bad choices in allowing his kids to act as judges when they weren't up to it.

At this point, the people approached Samuel and said that they were done with judges. They now wanted a king like all the other nations had. Samuel reminded them that if they had a king, they would be giving a lot of authority to that king, which could get bad. It's a lot harder to remove a king's authority, he told them, even if he takes your sons off to war or makes your daughters into servants. You will be giving the king your best land, your best crops and animals, and a lot more control over your lives. Are you sure you want to give someone that much authority over you? First Samuel 8:19–20 records their response: "But the people refused to listen to the voice of Samuel; they said, 'No! but we are determined to have a king over us, so that we also may be like other nations, and that our king may govern us and go out before us and fight our battles.'" Samuel appointed a king to rule over them with authority because the people asked for it, and God said that if that's what they wanted, that's what they'd get.

The point to all this is that authority is given. And that's exactly how the Bible as we know it became authoritative. Over time, people who lived in the years after Jesus began to recognize their own struggles, hardships, and questions being described in certain writings. Many of these writings and letters openly and authentically connected with their own fights with Rome, as well as their experiences of oppression, poverty, and injustice. These words spoke anew of God's presence and God's promise for the world. Some of these writings came into existence decades after Jesus and pointed to him as God's anointed one, the Messiah (Christ). Some books contained references to things Jesus was reported to have taught about God's priorities for the world. Others referred to followers of Jesus being inspired to advance God's work of justice and compassion in the world. Some of them connected the Jewish Scriptures directly to this Jesus in ways that helped them understand God's kingdom on a deeper and more relevant level. As these small communities grew in their trust of how Jesus and the Hebrew God addressed their difficult lives in ways that offered hope, these writings were granted more and more authority. If Jesus could be trusted to reveal that God's long-promised kingdom included them even when both the Roman and Jewish authorities said otherwise, then the writings that spoke of this could be trusted in other aspects as well. As these writings claimed that not even death could stop Jesus from revealing God's loving kingdom of peace, then they continued to be granted more authority around matters of life which kept falling short of God's kingdom. We can trust these writings, we can trust Jesus of Nazareth and the good news he taught, and we can trust God. The authority of some of these texts kept growing while others lost authority over time. Various church councils in the fourth and fifth centuries were convened to argue the merits of many different writings and which were most authoritative. This was the beginning of what Christians call the New Testament. Over time, particular books were gathered together and declared by portions of the church to be authoritative in their proclamation of truth about God.

Yet even that declaration was problematic. Differences of opinion were rampant, reflecting the early church's diversity in experience and perspective. Not to mention that during the fourth century the organized followers of Jesus in the West had become fast partners with the empire of Rome. According to some historians, it wasn't until the Quinisext Council of Trullo in 692 that the canonized list of books endorsed by the Western church was approved in Constantinople.[8] The particular books that these now institutional church leaders declared to be authoritative revealed as much about the religio-political world of early Europe as they did about the events described in those books.

8. Marsden, "When Was the Bible Finally Canonized?," para. 1.

The authority the Bible has been granted by many Christians today was long in coming and wasn't deemed urgent in the first several centuries of the church. The authority of the church evolved from oral stories in the lives of gathered Jesus communities to the hierarchy of an institutionalized political church. Several centuries went by before anything resembling the biblical authority we now know emerged through debated political church conventions. The final list of authoritative books of the Bible was still up for a vote as recently as the 1545 Council of Trent.

All this is merely to point out that the authority of Scripture has been somewhat relative. The recent development of literal interpretations as authoritative doesn't necessarily allow for the nuances, debates, and struggles through which Christianity has fought in deciding how and why the Bible is authoritative. Any level of scriptural authority is determined by the actual readers and the extent of their trust in those passages. Not to mention those readers' own experience, background, culture, faith journey, church upbringing, and biases.

The authority of the Bible can be problematic if not downright polarizing. However, when viewed in the light of the connecting nature and character of the Divine, it may be less so. Stories of encounters, discoveries, engagements, amazements, disappointments, and confusions with God can resonate deeply among us. As we continue seeking our purpose in our own time and place, the Bible can open for us a connection with the Divine exactly as it has done for others in history. In our common search for meaning and ultimate truth, Scripture can connect us across centuries and cultures as we learn from those who've struggled before us. We can share with one another how these biblical truths open our hearts and minds to new ways of encountering the God who is central in these stories. In so doing, perhaps we will be brought closer to each other in our various interpretations and perspectives, learning, growing, and connecting through an even broader and deeper awareness of the Divine.

For Discussion

1. Would you describe the Bible as "true"? If so, what does that mean for you? If not, what significance—if any—does the Bible have for you?

2. How do you read Scripture? As more of a novel? An operator's handbook? A series of laws or doctrines to be obeyed? A fallible human book with important ideas? God speaking directly to humanity? How might your particular view of Scripture limit or enhance your understanding of it?

3. This chapter describes the difference between specific historical facts and a deeper sense of truth. How might a broader understanding of truth help you in interpreting difficult Bible passages, e.g., "The Slaughter of the Innocents" in Matthew 2? What is at stake for you?

4. How much authority does the Bible have for you? Why?

CHAPTER 4

Division

Grocery Community

MY LEAST FAVORITE HOUSEHOLD chore is grocery shopping. My dislike of this task compels me to put it off for as long as possible. I'll eat everything in the house before I go to the grocery store. After all, expiration dates are merely suggestions, right?

I was at that point a while ago, so a trip to the supermarket became necessary. Though not a great chef by any means, one dish that I make well is a specific recipe for chicken fajitas.[1] They take more preparation than I usually like, but I really don't mind because they are one of my favorite things to eat. Every trip to the store includes the ingredients for this particularly fabulous dish.

I went over the list and saw that everything I needed for this recipe was included. I ordered everything and, at the appointed time, picked up the huge load of groceries.[2] As I put away my accrued plunder, I believed I had yet again attained the unattainable, acquiring the riches of a full refrigerator as a result. I felt the same level of pride that must have been experienced by Ottoman Sultan

1. Homolka, *Skinnytaste One & Done*, 80–82.

2. The technological development of ordering groceries online has likely kept me from starving.

Mehmed II himself, who in 1453 led the only successful siege on the impenetrable city of Constantinople. Yes, in my conquest of the grocery shopping task, I too had conquered the unconquerable (I really don't like grocery shopping).

A few days after my great grocery victory, I pulled all the ingredients for my favorite chicken fajitas and came to the horrible realization that I had forgotten to buy, of all things, the chicken. Defeated, I resigned myself to face my humiliation, go back to the grocery store, and meekly pick up a package of chicken breasts. I went directly to the meat counter, grabbed a one-pound package, and headed to the cashier. All experienced shoppers make it their goal to find the shortest checkout lane, which also requires watching for the fastest cashiers. Everyone is jockeying for position like we're in the Indy 500.

I settled in and was satisfied that no other line seemed to have an advantage. At that point, the person in front of me, with an overflowing grocery cart, saw my single poultry item. They unexpectedly invited me to step in front of them in the line, which I did with much gratitude. Yes, I would win the grocery store checkout race that day.

That gracious customer understood that shoppers connect as a temporary grocery store community. This person's concern wasn't just for themselves and how quickly they could get through the checkout. They were aware of the needs of the people around them and did something they didn't have to do, something no one expected them to do. They allowed me as a member of this temporary community to step in front of them. That act would delay them only by a few seconds but would save me considerably more time. Connected communities consider the benefit of the whole beyond merely the individuals.

There's a difference between individuals and communities. Communities look out for each other. Because we were in this grocery community together, it was possible to make decisions that benefit the whole rather than separate individuals. Community is more than a bunch of people in the same place fighting for position to get out of the store as quickly as possible. Community is connection. Community reveals the image of God and is therefore our default setting.

Winning

We have falsely come to believe that "winning" as individuals is the epitome of the human experience. Getting through the checkout line faster, receiving a larger paycheck, getting a promotion in the workplace, and driving a faster car are all part of our American culture. These individual accomplishments are valued and rewarded among us. Through individual effort and perseverance, the cultural goal is for each person to do what is necessary to advance and win—even if that means that someone else must fall behind and lose.

This pervasive attitude is culturally present in all parts of our lives, including our approach to church, faith, righteousness, holiness, and more. For most churches in our society, the goal isn't to live as a collective community valuing the perspective, history, and story of each one gathered. Nor is it to contribute to a greater whole in the image of God. It's not even to live this connecting nature of the Divine in the broader community. Rather, much more effort is put into individual congregations winning by being larger, having more money, developing better programs, hiring more charismatic staff than the next church. If our church is bigger than your church, we win.

Individually, this religiously competitive attempt to win the closeness-to-God contest is also accomplished by separating ourselves from others. When we believe we can become closer to God than someone else, we have stepped fully into self-righteousness. The one who follows their particular doctrines and rules most closely wins the righteousness challenge. Therefore, it becomes merely optional to help, accompany, or listen to those of lesser righteousness. I only have to be better than you. It is no coincidence that too many of us prefer the dogmatic doctrines and interpretations that make it easier to justify our own righteousness over someone else's.

Denominationally, if we can claim that our doctrines and confessions are better than another's or our interpretation of Scripture is godlier, we win. Devotees of a specific church polity will declare their policies and traditions draw them closer to God than others' (according to their own internal interpretation), and therefore allow them to claim they are more righteous than others. Coming close to God winds up being a contest of doctrinal justification that can be won or lost rather than living as connected people in the image of God. We are continually checking to make sure our ecclesial checkout line is fastest.

Shortcuts

As we continue to ignore the divine connecting lessons revealed through physics, biology, sociology, astronomy, psychology, chemistry, and theology, not to mention our created nature, we bypass our default setting of connecting relationship. The need to bond with something larger than us has been hardwired into us from the beginning of creation. As long as individual winning continues to have cultural rewards, we'll always be searching for quicker and more convenient ways to claim a relationship with God. So far, even these best efforts have been superficial movements resulting in division rather than connection. A constant thread through much of human history has been our counterproductive efforts to discover shortcuts in achieving a connection to God and our perceived purpose within creation. Because these efforts are individualized at the outset, they are doomed to fall short. They can only serve to separate us from God and each other. But that hasn't stopped us from putting significant energy into them.

On this score of division, the Christian church certainly holds its own with every other agency, institution, or government. Historically, we appropriated the Divinity that holds all things and connects all things, then labeled our limited version of this unifying connection as "the one true God." We created characteristics of God that, coincidentally, provide and maintain power among us within the church, separating the church from everything else.

Do you want to know God? Well, we in the church have the best (and the only true) answers to that. We'll create a list of ways you can get closer to God, even the ways you can be with God into all eternity. Follow our rules of belief, and you can be among the righteous few who are closer to God and may even live with God forever in paradise. If that doesn't motivate you to follow us and adhere to our teachings, there's always the threat of eternal hellfire and suffering—which we, with our self-declared superior doctrinal positions, can help you avoid.

The quest to separate ourselves and rise above those outside the church has led the historic church to lay claim to being the winners in God's name. In planting its victory flag in the territory of righteousness, the church has declared itself an institution separate from the rest of the world, the only one with an inside track to the Divine. This triumphal assertion foundationally opposes the nature and character of the unifying nature of God, which holds all things in connective unity. Rather than providing a perspective about joining creation in a relationship with the Divine as revealed through Jesus, the church has separated itself as the only winner in a competition for eternity.

Prescription

As the ones who claim to know God best, the church has historically declared that you will need to believe certain things that we have come to trust are true. These beliefs will be rewarded with recognition, an eased conscience, a sense of righteousness, and eternal life in heaven. If you accomplish a high enough level of piety in proclaiming these beliefs, you can even attain sainthood and be canonized as a model for others to follow. The ultimate express lane to eternal bliss. Listen to us, the church declares, and God will look on you with favor. Don't, and you'll be lost forever. Don't question, don't poke or prod, just accept. Win or lose. Heaven or hell. God or Satan. Righteousness or evil. Everlasting joy or eternal suffering. And only we in the church have the certainty of prescribed truths that can put you on the fast track to this ultimate individual victory.

To hold power and maintain propriety in the arena of righteousness, the church had to figure out who was in and who was out, who were the spiritual winners and who were the losers, who had the direct access to God and who was lost. To aid this, the church developed prescribed doctrines, creeds, catechisms, rituals, and traditions for just that purpose.

It's not the intent of this book to debate the merits of any of these historical documents. Without a doubt, these teachings have helped, and in many cases continue to help people in their connection with the Divine. The authority that these traditions were originally granted, however, had more to do with "us" claiming a more complete and truthful knowledge of God than "you." Because we claim to understand God better, we are more righteous, godlier, and, in effect, better than you. In separating ourselves from others who have a lesser or even a false theology, we believe that the church can now specify with certainty a way to connect more closely to God than others. In separating ourselves from those outside the church, we have professed that we have risen above them, discovering the godly shortcut to a connection with the Divine. This is the trap of separation that we continually fall into—countering the very nature of God in which we are created.

Among the most prominent and influential doctrinal prescriptions of the church are its creeds, which provide examples of the church's attempts to separate itself from those outside its godly boundaries. The Apostles' Creed, with roots going back to the late second century, served as one of the first broad attempts to unify the followers of Christ under one umbrella of approved beliefs. Articulated in Rome during a rather tumultuous time in the church there, it brought together a disparate group of bishops in a unifying statement of faith. This was an important step in coming together on such things as baptism, who has authority to lead the church, and how to summarize the message of Scripture. Though its origins are not completely clear, the document was finalized in the eighth century and again clarified which beliefs were true and which were false as the church sought to separate itself from heresy within its own ranks. Correct beliefs as prescribed in the Apostles' Creed were considered the way to come to God, rather than serving as a communal connection to God and all creation.

The formulation of the Nicene Creed in the fourth century primarily provided a way to separate the church from the theology of Arianism, which questioned the eternal divinity of Jesus. It thereby established the only correct view of God in the utilization of a Trinitarian formula. God was now officially three-in-one, Father, Son, and Holy Spirit. This core belief was a necessary entry point in gaining access to God. Again, doctrinal shortcuts superseded the nature of God. Ironically, the doctrine of the Trinity itself claims that the one God is connection and relationship among the three persons. Without realizing it, the church of the fourth century created a doctrine that stated the very relational nature of God, but used it to separate the church from the rest of society.

Later doctrines, teachings, and traditions all built upon the direction of early statements. These attempts to bring us closer to God through individual understanding and knowledge led us to separate ourselves from non-Christian people, who are also created in the divine image. The quest for self-proclaimed certainty about who and what God is became a higher priority than experiencing the connection to one another that is characteristic of the Divine.

As stated previously, much of these officially articulated statements originated from the church's desire to help people connect to God. Throughout most of its history the church has regrettably erred on the side of desiring certainty about God over living in the image of God. The result has been the limiting of the church in its ability to achieve its original goal of bringing people closer to God. In its quest for a prescription of certainty, the church came to believe they alone held the inside information on the Divine. However, it soon became an exercise in power and control. Separation and individualism generally lead to power struggles, to winning at the expense of connecting, and attempted shortcuts that wind up being a detour away from the nature of God.

The Gospel of Luke describes one of many incidents where a doctrinal stance was exposed as contrary to the nature of the Divine. In chapter 6, Jesus cures a man with a withered hand, allowing him to return and reconnect to his community, now whole and righteous. The church leaders were furious because Jesus prioritized restoration to policy, wholeness to tradition.

> On another Sabbath he entered the synagogue and taught, and there was a man there whose right hand was withered. The scribes and the Pharisees were watching him to see whether he would cure on the Sabbath, so that they might find grounds to bring an accusation against him. But he knew what they were thinking, and he said to the man who had the withered hand, "Come and stand in the middle." He got up and stood there. Then Jesus said to them, "I ask you, is it lawful to do good or to do harm on the Sabbath, to save life or to destroy it?" After looking around at all of them, he said to him, "Stretch out your hand." He did so, and his hand was restored. But they were filled with fury and began discussing with one another what they might do to Jesus. (Luke 6:6–11)

We look at this miracle and wonder how those religious leaders in that day could be so callous. After all, the man was healed! How could that not take precedence over a Sabbath regulation? First of all, it's not that simple. People in the church largely haven't kept Sabbath law for a couple thousand years, so it's rather easy for us to write off this rule as trite and irrelevant.

Secondly, the Sabbath laws were originally given to provide life. The commandment to remember the Sabbath day in Exodus 20:8–11 comes from the creation story in Genesis, where God rested on the seventh day and blessed it. God's people are to rest on this day because it is in the image of God.

Additionally, in Deuteronomy, the Sabbath law is tied to the people being released from slavery in Egypt (Deuteronomy 5:12–15). Pharaoh demanded that the Hebrew slaves keep making more and more bricks, under harsher and harsher conditions. Slaves cannot take a day off; free people can. Thus, when their descendants refrain from working every Sabbath, they are to recall that God delivered them from slavery.

We need to be careful we're not casually acquiescing to what may be antisemitic attitudes due to a lack of understanding regarding a practice in which Christians no longer participate. The Sabbath laws to Jews in Jesus' day were real, significant, holy, and a connection to a righteous God. This scene in Luke's Gospel wasn't intended to make the Pharisees look trivial and petty. Luke related this story because Sabbath observance was a significant issue for the early followers of Jesus. This was not Jesus disregarding Sabbath as marginal. It was the early church figuring out how much of the image of God was revealed in Jesus and how much was revealed in the Sabbath laws. In a difficult struggle, Luke's Jesus insisted that helping, healing, and restoring to community were divine acts, fully in keeping with the original intent of the Sabbath laws of giving life.

Life and community relationships were made real by Jesus' healing the man on the Sabbath. When confronted with laws and doctrines that may seem to counter that, we would do well to look at church regulations and traditions through that lens. It's too simple to hide behind a church policy without considering whether that policy restricts life and connection to community. If the confession of a creedal statement gives life in a particular context, wonderful. If it serves to separate insiders from outsiders or specify a set of beliefs necessary to be included, that is problematic. Many church leaders and church members today discourage, if not outright refuse, life-giving community to people they consider less righteous. LGBTQIA+ people are too often denied acceptance in a church community and are told that they must repent of their "sinfulness" before they can be welcomed. In my own denomination, the Evangelical Lutheran Church in America, our siblings of color often relate that many of our traditions and practices push them out to the edges of the church, keeping us the Whitest denomination in the United States.

A Life of Its Own

One justified criticism of mainline Christian denominations is a lack of vibrant spirituality. To advance that point, there are some traditions that know and practice their rituals and traditions flawlessly but still lack a significant connection to the Divine. Too often, churches spend their primary energy dealing with doctrinal questions as opposed to connecting ones. Are clergy required to wear clerical collars? Do those who lead in gathered worship need to wear certain churchly garb? Must songs and hymns be only from approved sources—not coincidentally that denomination's own publishing house? Is Communion efficacious if the person receiving it is under a certain age or hasn't received certain instruction? How many candles? Can women be ordained? How long is the procession? How serious a faux pas are we committing if we mistakenly slip in an "alleluia" during Lent? Are percussion instruments sanctified? Are LGBTQIA+ people fully included? Can we mandate that crying babies be removed from community worship into an isolated nursery, where they won't distract the rest of us from our individual piety?

Then there are the everyday pragmatic questions. Do we have the money to fix the roof? Will hiring a youth director bring the young families back to church? Should the secretary have that much control over church policy? It's understandable that churches can get lost in a never-ending list of tasks that require constant attention. But none of this fulfills our purpose and should not receive our primary energy and effort. If kept in proper perspective, many of these questions can move us along in our purpose, but only if that mission is honestly clarified first.

A dialogue on many of these questions can, in fact, help people connect spiritually to the Divine. Discerning how some of these issues help or hinder the divine role of the church needs some care and consideration. The problem isn't necessarily the rites, procedures, traditions, and doctrines. The problem comes when we offer these as having a life of their own and allow them to replace the deeper work of genuinely connecting to God and to each other.

The original purpose of the Christian church as a community was to proclaim and live the connecting image of God in the world as revealed by Jesus of Nazareth. That seems to have long been lost. That purpose has been replaced with unnecessary busy work and a prescribed way to separate ourselves from the rest of the world through individual beliefs, practices, and knowledge. We are assured that when we do all this, we will rise above those who don't, thus bringing us even closer to God than everyone else. We've come to believe that we must separate ourselves from those who are below us, who are less righteous, so we can connect to the God who is above us. And nothing is further from the image of God than that.

For Discussion

1. In what areas of your life do you find yourself most compelled to "win"? What would happen if you approached those areas differently?

2. When in your life have you considered your own theology/church/beliefs as "winning" against the competition for divine favor? Do you still hold that view? If not, what aspects of your current belief system do you now consider to be superior (by the way, proclaiming "I believe all beliefs are valid" may still be an attempt to win a belief competition)?

3. Are you more comfortable with a doctrinal view of God or an experiential one? What are the benefits and drawbacks of each?

4. By definition, the idea of winning includes the idea that others are losing. The theological assumption of someone losing often indicates a lack of understanding of their beliefs. Make a point of getting to know someone with a different belief system than yours. Find out why they hold those beliefs and why they work for them. This is not a competition to see whose theology is best, but an exercise in connection, understanding, and community.

CHAPTER 5

Brokenness

Othering

IN THE LAST TWO years I've lived in three different cities, each in a different state. It's hard not to notice how different the drivers are from one city to another. In my observation, Denver drivers are aggressive, Las Cruces drivers are oblivious, and Park City drivers are entitled. Though untrue, it's still easy to make those generalizations, to categorize the drivers because I'm not originally from these cities. I'm different than they are and consider myself to be a better driver than them because I don't believe I drive like they do.

The point being that it is tempting to categorize everyone into handy groups to differentiate them from me. Obviously not all Denver drivers are aggressive, yet it's convenient to label all people in Denver that way. It separates them from people like me, who are nothing but polite on the road. If everyone drove like me, there would be far fewer accidents on our highways. Despite the traffic tickets I've received, this is what I keep telling myself.

Whether it's driving style or any other descriptor, we share that tendency to justify ourselves as different from others, by which we specifically mean we're better than them. "They" are all the same in Denver so, because they aren't like "us," they are much more of a danger when speeding down the interstate. When we can keep them in a separate driving category from us, we can make judgments about them without the hard work of getting to know them, taking a ride in their car with them, or discovering possible reasons for their driving habits.

Kendra Cherry, in a January 23, 2023 article in the mental health online publication *Verywell Mind*, identifies this way of thinking as "othering," a phenomenon in which some individuals or groups are defined and labeled as not fitting in within the norms of a social group.[1] Othering is the opposite of communal belonging. Whereas belonging denotes acceptance and inclusion, othering indicates intolerance and exclusion. Long ago, it may have been necessary for people to define the boundaries between friends and enemies. But for most of us this practice is no longer about survival in our daily lives. Othering has much more to do with power, justification, and separation than anything else.

Generally, we other those about whom we know very little. This lack of personal knowledge and contact with people can lead to assumptions about them, which makes it easier to perceive them as overwhelmingly different. Cherry writes,

> Also known as in-group favoritism, this is a psychological tendency to favor one's own in-group over members of out-groups. . . . Other factors such as self-identity and social identity also play a role in this favoritism. In-group bias often influences how we evaluate others, how we treat them, and how we share our resources with them.[2]

Being part of a group that is separated from others can have a significant impact on the behaviors and identities of those who identify with that group.

The act of othering drivers in various cities, although usually unkind and untrue, isn't likely to do any permanent damage in and of itself. It does, however, reveal a mindset in opposition to the divine nature of connectivity. When people see themselves belonging

1. Cherry, "What Is Othering?," para. 1.
2. Cherry, "What Is Othering?," paras. 15–17.

to a certain social group, they tend to discriminate and can even engage in hostile behavior toward people who are not members of that group. This act of separation makes us more likely to invoke harm as it becomes increasingly easier to perceive others as not just different, but less worthy, or even less human. A simple motive for separating ourselves is to be able to claim our innate goodness as opposed to others. In so doing, we continue the pattern of othering to dehumanize those who are different than us. This allows us to further distance ourselves from them, which reduces our empathy for them. The further separated they are, the more easily we can see them as less human, less worthy of compassion and understanding. Carried further, othering can result in pushing those separated into the marginal edges of culture. There they will face even more hardships and even wider separation through disparities in economics, housing, criminal justice, education, and healthcare. On a societal level this act of separating "them" from "us" can lead to justified discrimination and legal policies that demonize people who are considered different or less deserving. This has been used as a means of control by those in positions of political leadership by exploiting those fears and anxieties about the other. As a result, minorities can be made out to be enemies and people can then further justify dehumanizing policies, sometimes with deadly consequences. It's fairly evident that most of the horrible acts in the world are carried out as acts of extreme othering. Historical villains have a consistent record of degrading those they don't know, who appear different, or who may pose some imagined threat. The concentration camps of World War II and the recent rise in American antisemitic rhetoric and violence are prime examples of the hatred and evil that are again being unleashed in extreme othering. Othering is brokenness. Separation opposes the image of God.

You Have Made Them Equal to Us

There is a parable in the Gospel of Matthew that exposes our propensity for othering those we consider different or of less value. In this story, commonly known as "The Laborers in the Vineyard," Jesus is again trying to describe what the ways of God are like. He compares the reign of God to a generous landowner who needs to hire temporary workers for his farm. He goes into town early in the morning and finds people looking for work. He hires them, agreeing to pay them fairly for a full day's work. He goes back to the town square several more times during the day, each time hiring more people to work and agreeing to pay them fairly.

At the end of the day, he lines them up to receive their wages. Those who were hired last and who had only worked for an hour receive a full day's pay. Those who worked the entire day become excited, thinking that since they've worked longer, they are entitled to much more in wages. Yet they receive the same—a full day's pay for a full day's work. They go to the landlord and complain about how unfair this is, yet the landlord counters by assuring them they have been treated with all fairness, reminding them, "Did you not agree with me for the usual daily wage?" What I pay others has no bearing on your worth or the quality of your work.

The complaint of unfairness had very little to do with the full day's wage workers were paid. Instead, it was about the later workers getting paid the same amount. The specific protest to the landowner was that he had "made *them* equal to *us*" (emphasis added).[3]

That kind of undeserved generosity seemed wrong to those who felt they were entitled to more pay than others. The infraction, they believed, was that the landlord didn't categorize the later workers differently than those hired early. It was deemed offensive that all were treated equally regardless of perceived privilege or entitlement. The image of God doesn't distinguish between "them" (whoever they are) and "us" (whoever we are). No separation, no othering. We are all connected, all equally worthy in the divine image.

Over and over again, the Gospels describe Jesus making connections and relationships, crossing many cultural, sexual, religious, and ethnic boundaries to do so. Despite Jesus consistently

---

3. It is worthwhile to read this very pointed parable in Matthew 20:1–16.

pointing out that God's ways are the ways of connection, empathy, and love for others, those in the church continue to find ways to declare separation. "They" then become different, less worthy, less human, less godly. They can now be defined as sinful. Once we declare others to be wicked and evil, it's a small step to support deeper separation by pushing them even further down in society. For everyone's good, we will need to eradicate them in the name of God for the protection of all godly people. It has been a consistent theme, including the entire history of this country. Consider a few ugly portions of our American past and present culture.

The Doctrine of Discovery

According to the Cornell Law School's Legal Information In-stitute, the doctrine of discovery refers to "a principle in public international law under which, when a nation 'discovers' land, it directly acquires rights on that land."[4] No surprise that this doc-trine has its roots in the church. A papal decree by Pope Nicholas V in 1452 specifically sanctioned and encouraged the European conquest, colonization, and exploitation of non-Christian terri-tories and peoples.

In 1792 Thomas Jefferson declared that the doctrine of discovery was international, and therefore was applicable to the newly formed U.S. government. Under the rules of war, when the United States won its independence from Great Britain, it took control of the land previously declared to be owned by King George under the doctrine.

Later, the doctrine of discovery became a legal precedent used to prevent indigenous people from owning land in the Unites States. In the 1770s, Illinois and Piankeshaw Indians sold land in what is now the state of Illinois to a man named Thomas Johnson. After American independence, the U.S. government assumed control of huge areas of land west of the thirteen colo-nies, which included Johnson's parcels. Later, the same land was

---

4. Legal Information Institute, "Doctrine of Discovery," para. 1.

purchased from the government by William McIntosh. Johnson sued McIntosh, saying he had already purchased the land from the original native owners prior to the war. In the court case of Johnson v. McIntosh, the Supreme Court under Chief Justice John Marshall upheld the McIntosh family's ownership of land purchased from the federal government. He reasoned that since the federal government now controlled the land, the Indians had only a "right of occupancy" and held no title to the land. They'd never had the right to sell land to Johnson because they were unable to own land belonging to the U.S. government, even though the government had taken control years later. "Marshall based the decision on the 'Discovery Doctrine.'"[5]

Many American children grew up learning that this continent had been discovered by Christopher Columbus, as if the land had been unoccupied before he arrived. The indigenous inhabitants were considered less than the European Christian explorers. This racism and cultural superiority based on the doctrine of discovery has been used to justify all manner of violence, including the attempted genocide of entire native nations.

Hundreds of years of decisions and laws based on the doctrine of discovery continue to negatively impact Native Americans to this day. Laws are still in existence that invalidate or ignore the rights, sovereignty, and humanity of indigenous peoples here and around the world. In the United States, that legacy of separation and domination is reflected in an endless series of broken treaties, resulting in the stolen sovereignty of our indigenous communities. The U.S. government continues its assertions of power over the tribes. We see this lived out through ongoing injustices in water rights, oil and mineral extraction on Native lands, and border and immigration policies that negatively affect tribal communities.

The land on which I am living as I write this was taken from the Eastern Shoshone and Ute nations.[6] Though complicated and full of ethical and logistical challenges, Native tribes are attempting to

5. "1823: Supreme Court Rules."

6. According to the address look-up tool on the homepage of *Native Land Digital*.

educate about and bring appreciation to a historical understanding of land and property. The bottom line, however, is that the United States along with many other countries around the world have utilized laws and policies such as the doctrine of discovery to unethically acquire land. Dehumanizing the land's original inhabitants in the name of God and civilization to gain property and resources violates the very nature of God and the created order. Othering is brokenness. Separation opposes the image of God.

White Supremacy

Memphis, Tennessee is the birthplace of the Blues. Historic Beale Street, quiet during the day, transforms into a busy, loud festival of music and food as the sun sets. Memphis is also the location of the National Civil Rights Museum, which is housed primarily in the refurbished Lorraine Hotel—the site of the assassination of Martin Luther King Jr. on April 4, 1968.

Calling this museum "important" or "well presented" is inadequate at best. It most certainly is that, but more, it is living history, told through voices that are often separate and left out in school textbooks or in the chambers of power. After enduring centuries of forced migration, African Americans even now continue to struggle for equality in their own country.

I had the opportunity to visit this landmark museum a few years ago. What resonated with me in the National Civil Rights Museum were the tones of fear that have always been associated with Whites losing power over any group of others. The terror caused by the possibility of Blacks being seen as equal to Whites is invariably followed up with statements made throughout our history to deny or even justify policies and actions based on that fear. Among the accepted historical slogans are: "Slavery is a time-honored American tradition"; "It's for their own good"; "We gave them citizenship and the vote (the 14th and 15th Amendments, passed after the Civil War), yet it's still not enough"; "The Supreme Court supported 'Jim Crow' laws, so they are the laws of the land"; "Separate but equal is the best policy"; "They won't take over our schools"; "Race riots wouldn't happen if those people would just settle down"; and even the more recent "All Lives Matter."

As I moved through exhibit after exhibit, I was led through American history from the perspective of marginalized people whose voices have been largely ignored. I heard voices of people captured and enslaved as early as 1619. I heard the cries of slaves over a period of three hundred years in the United States. I heard the early recognition that the revered phrase "all men are created equal" did not include "all men [sic]." I heard voices of persistence and courage in dealing with chronic, culturally embedded injustices. I heard creative attempts at calling for freedom, rights, and decency for all people. I heard cries for education, for housing, and for employment, the historic denial of which was somehow justified. I heard heroic voices demanding change and frightened voices clinging to the status quo. I heard voices on strike, voices being beaten, voices lynched, voices favoring violence, voices bent on vengeance, voices denied, voices ignored, voices suppressed. But the voices continued. And still continue. And they are, as yet, not always heard.

This is because the response to these unheard and uncomfortable voices—not only in history, but today—are perspectives that come from fear, denial, and self-justification. Longing to maintain isolating power, those behind these fearful views deny the legitimacy of stories other than their own, stories that reveal the continued and systemic abuse of that power.

On that same trip, I took a train from Memphis to Jackson, Mississippi and visited the new Mississippi Civil Rights Museum, which had opened only the year before. This museum is different than the National Civil Rights Museum in Memphis in a couple of ways. One, it focuses on civil rights events specifically in Mississippi. Two, it is bolder, more direct, and somehow more passionate.

Even the architecture and design add to the effect in Jackson. One of the most striking features for me is toward the end. The path through the museum eventually leads into a wide but oddly angular corridor. There are crowded displays along the walls, but inescapably down the center in a straight row are multiple flat black glass columns, each about ten feet high and about eighteen inches wide. Front and back, they list the name, date, and race of every lynching victim in the state's history. Column after column, hundreds upon hundreds of names of human beings who were tortured, beaten, hung, killed. The violence depicted on these panels is sickening. That corridor of unbelievable cruelty is unavoidable. Which, I assume, is the point.

How can that level of evil, brutality, and hatred ever be justified? How can anyone possibly believe that centuries of violent bloodshed and torment are redeemable in any fashion? These tortuous lynchings, these vile murders, are what is possible when we continue separating people into racial categories rather than recognizing the connectivity of all humanity.

Racial othering is not just something awful from our past. The ramifications of a history of enslaving people in this country are still very present. Policies are still in place, and are still being written, to ensure the continued separation of Blacks from Whites, including voting rights, criminal justice, property ownership, and more. Othering is brokenness. Separation opposes the image of God.

Immigration

At the beginning of the presidential campaign of 2016, one candidate for that office deliberately and maliciously othered Mexican, Central American, and South American people seeking refuge in the United States, making sure to categorize them as despicable people who need to be separated. "When Mexico sends its people, they're not sending their best. They're not sending you. They're not sending you. They're sending people that have lots of problems, and they're bringing those problems with us. They're bringing drugs. They're bringing crime. They're rapists. And some, I assume, are good people."[7]

7. Donald Trump, presidential announcement speech, June 16, 2015.

This harmful othering contributes to ongoing violence and cruel immigration policies related to the U.S. southern border. Families separated, children lost, people placed in cages to keep "them" separate from "us." The refusal to consider any kind of immigration reform is based on the fear of them being made equal to us. The paralysis that prevents any compassionate revision of cruel policies runs counter to a consistent biblical witness of the inclusion of and care for immigrants.

For more than a year I lived less than fifty miles from the U.S./Mexican border. During that time, I had the privilege of serving on the board of directors for Border Servant Corps, an organization that exists to promote and demonstrate "justice, kindness, and humility through the intentional exploration of community, simplicity, social justice, and spirituality in the U.S./México border region."[8] The compassion exhibited by the staff and volunteers of BSC was inspiring. Each person seeking refuge in the U.S. or migrating across the border was treated with dignity and cared for in their full humanity. Resources were collected collaboratively from across the country and distributed equitably to all who needed them to help them relocate safely and legally within the borders of the United States. Organizations such as Border Servant Corp reveal the divine image of connected unity shared by all people regardless of language, heritage, country of origin, religion, or political affiliation.

Recognition of this connectivity across geopolitical boundaries was among the first laws governing the Hebrew people, newly freed from slavery in Egypt, and which identified them as people of God. Living as God's people and revealing the nature of their God to the other nations meant that they would always provide special care for vulnerable travelers and aliens residing among them.[9] Othering is brokenness. Separation opposes the image of God.

8. Border Servant Corp, "Our Mission," lines 1–3.

9. Exodus 22:21; 23:9; Leviticus 23:35, 47; Deuteronomy 14:29; 26:13, among many others.

LGBTQIA+

Even as I write this, some state and local governments are attempting to draft (and in some cases passing) harmful legislation dehumanizing those who are anything other than straight, White, cisgender male, evangelical Christians. Laws separating transgender people, especially teenagers, are life-threatening. Denying affirming healthcare, requiring hormonal testing for suspected trans athletes, imposing humiliating and nonsensical bathroom regulations, implementing "Don't Say Gay" laws that deny the humanity—even the existence—of LGBTQ individuals and all the other dehumanizing policies in portions of this country stand in stark opposition to the divine nature in which all are created. The othering of those in the LGBTQ community, based entirely on fear of those whom the straight White majority have separated, has led to hateful legislation that is detrimental to us all. Othering is brokenness. Separation opposes the image of God.

"I Have No Idea Why It's Still That Way."

On my last day in Jackson, Mississippi during the aforementioned trip through the Southern United States, I had a conversation with a young Black woman that will remain embedded in my memory. She was a very hospitable employee in the hotel where I was staying, and over the course of my time there we had struck up a few conversations. The last time I spoke with her I wondered out loud if she would answer a question for me. "I find Mississippi somewhat bewildering." I continued. "This state has the highest percentage of Black people in the country, and yet . . ." I faltered.

"And yet we're the reddest of the red states?" she suggested.

"Well, maybe. It's just that there have been really brutal aspects of history regarding race here, yet there have also been astonishingly bold stands on civil rights and human rights."

"I don't get it, either," she replied. "I'm bewildered too. With all the Black civil rights heroes that have come from Mississippi, I don't understand why there hasn't been more change." She paused, looked around, leaned a little closer, and spoke very quietly. "For instance, in this hotel, virtually all of the service employees are Black, but every person in management is White. I have no idea why it's still that way."

I will always be grateful to this brave young woman for speaking to a White male stranger with such clarity about the reality of being othered, of being separated, of being considered less worthy. Othering is brokenness. Separation is the opposite of the image of God.

For Discussion

1. "Othering" is defined in this chapter as individuals or groups being separated by a more powerful majority due to differences from that majority's norm. Have you ever had the experience of being othered? Whether your experience was mild or extreme, describe how you were treated and how that felt.

2. What groups of people have you othered? How can you make reparations for that and form a more divine connection with that individual or group?

3. Several examples of extreme othering are given throughout this chapter. What else would you contribute to these examples, either through naming additional othered groups or further evidence of the harm done to groups when they are separated through othering?

4. Consider groups in your area that are known for standing against the brokenness of othering. How can you connect with them to have a stronger voice?

CHAPTER 6

Remnant

Rising from the Ashes

ONE OF THE BENEFITS of living in a house that's more than sixty years old is that the landscaping is well developed, particularly the trees. One of my favorites is a large ash tree in the corner of my backyard that, apparently, was planted when the house was first built in 1962. Because ash trees are versatile and abundant, they can grow in a variety of settings and environments. Forests of sixteen varieties of ash trees can be found in low wetlands, along streams, on the plains, as well as in mountainous areas. Ash trees in the United States and Canada are hardy, drought resistant, and handle environmental stresses well, so they have also been heavily planted in urban areas.

My ash is one of those suburban wonders; majestic, tall, and healthy—at least so far. With the continuing spread of the emerald ash borer (*Agrilus planipennis*), the most devastating insect ever to strike a North American tree, the long-term fate of my backyard tree is uncertain. Since the borer's discovery in 2002, it has killed hundreds of millions of ash trees across half the continent and caused tens of billions of dollars of damage.[1] The larvae kill trees by burrowing in and feeding on the bark, then destroying the tree's vascular system, which carries water and minerals from the roots up to the leaves and nutrients back down to the roots. Once these larvae have fed and are developed, they grow into adult beetles and fly off to lay eggs on the leaves of the next tree, and the cycle begins again. Once infected, very few of these grand trees survive.

But a tiny remnant of ash trees can fend off this deadly infestation. The U.S. Department of Agriculture has sponsored a study to try and discover why an occasional infected tree survives the ash borer. Forest geneticists are sampling thousands of ash trees, seeking the one in a thousand that kills the insects rather than being killed by them. Once that rare tree is discovered containing dead larvae, small branches are cut from it and grafted onto a non-infested tree so that a new generation from that resistant tree is grown. If the genetic secrets within this tiny minority of resistant trees can be passed on to new generations, there is hope that North American ash trees can avoid extinction. Like chestnuts, elms, and hemlocks, once a plague of fungus or insects begin attacking a certain genus of tree, it is likely doomed. In the case of the mighty ash, however, there is hope that reforestation may be possible within ten years.

Though I'm hopeful, the reality is that my backyard tree may not ultimately survive the emerald ash borer plague. But there is a remnant of trees that will. Whether through luck, science, or divine intervention, there always seems to be a remnant to carry on. This is true not only for trees, but for so many other aspects of our world. There continue to be remnants of lost cultures, eradicated ethnicities, former architectures, banned lifestyles, prohibited systems, and even overpowered church priorities that survive plagues, disasters, oppression, and misdirection. It has always been that way.

1. Popkin, "Rising from the Ashes," para. 2.

Covenant Theology

The survival of a remnant following some type of catastrophe is a common scriptural theme. A noticeable aspect is that throughout the Bible God often seems to take significant action to advance God's mission through many of these remnants. A catastrophe occurs (most often understood to be caused by the people turning away from God), a remnant survives, the saving action of God is appreciated afterwards, and a broader and deeper awareness of the Divine results. When the entirety of the biblical witness is looked at through this long lens of remnants, a thematic action of God can be seen. Through these remnant people or groups there is a consistent movement toward fuller inclusion, of furthering the connection among people and cultures to the Divine and to the world.

The Reformed tradition's covenant theology, first articulated in the sixteenth century, can be helpful as a tool to observe this. Briefly, Ligon Duncan summarizes covenant theology as "a framework for biblical interpretation . . . that recognizes that the redemptive history revealed in Scripture is explicitly articulated through a succession of covenants (Adam, Noah, Abraham, Moses, David, and New), thus providing an organizing principle for biblical theology."[2] Though my use of covenant theology isn't perfectly in keeping with orthodox Calvinist tradition, I nonetheless believe it to be useful as a framework through which remnant peoples are seen as revealing God's connecting, inclusive movement in history as recorded by biblical authors.

The overarching covenant of grace in this tradition is described as God's overall commitment to Adam to redeem a broken creation, the goal being to connect all aspects of creation back to God. Here, the divine movement toward the inclusion of all people unfolds through a series of covenants between God and God's people. Each covenant reveals a new remnant rising from the previous one, expanding the scope and inclusivity of divine connection.

The first in this series of covenants is referred to as the Noahic Covenant. Made between Noah, as the lone remnant of

2. Duncan, "Covenant Theology," para. 1.

righteousness left on earth, and God (Genesis 8:20—9:17) after the great flood that destroyed almost all life, God promises that the world will, in fact, survive. There will be life somehow. Specifics aren't given at this point, but a promise of life is made with a rainbow as the covenantal sign.

Building on that, the Abrahamic Covenant takes the promise of generic life given to Noah and begins to make it tangible. Through one unlikely remnant couple described in chapters 12–22 of Genesis as faithful to God, God promises to bless the whole world. Abram and Sarai become Abraham and Sarah, the patriarch and matriarch whose progeny will be plentiful, will have land, and will be formed into a nation. In the covenantal sign of circumcision, God's promise is that it will be through this nation that the world will be restored to its default connection with and to the Divine.

In the Mosaic Covenant, the descendants of Abraham and Sarah become a specific people among all people on Earth whose very life and identity is found in a covenantal relationship with God. Described in the book of Exodus as having been enslaved in Egypt for over four hundred years, these specific people are set free and given the Mosaic Law. They follow Moses through the wilderness to claim the land promised them, where they are to live in obedience to this covenant as a remnant people still existing in divine connection to one another and to God.

Following this is the Davidic Covenant. From among these people, God chooses the little shepherd boy David to be the king, through whom the ultimate savior of the world would come. As king, David begins to lead this nation in revealing the connecting nature of God to the nations, so that through them even those outside of the nation of Israel may see the nature of God. This remnant people, who are the leftovers of faithfulness, have an expansive purpose in this covenant, to reveal God to the rest of the world.

Finally comes the New Covenant, where God makes a connection to the Divine available to people everywhere in the life, ministry, death, and resurrection of Jesus. Though unfulfilled until "the end of the age," this is the ultimate covenant of expanding inclusion. It is here that the nature of the Divine is fulfilled for all creation, connected once and for all in the default design of the universe. The nature of God was somehow recognized through remnants who continue a natural journey of expanding connection. Disasters, disobedience, ignorance, disbelief, even treachery don't seem to be able to stop the default setting of mutual, reciprocal connection from arising in some remnant group. That same perspective of a remnant rising up in a new loving relationship is seen not just in covenant theology, but in many other aspects of life, culture, and history.

Prophetic Tradition

The role of Hebrew prophets as described in the Old Testament was not to predict the future, as is often thought. Rather, it was to name the existing disconnected reality and call people back to their connection to God based on a life defined by a covenant with God. This often defied the wishes of those in power because it inconveniently called them to act for the well-being of all the people as God's chosen nation rather than gaining more individual power. Wealth, riches, and dominance separated rulers from their subjects as opposed to connecting to them. The cry of the prophets often called out these forms of disconnecting power in favor of empathy with those who had become isolated in poverty and injustice.

The most potent messages from these prophets often followed some form of tragedy where disconnection from God was understood as the underlying cause. Let a remnant arise and be faithful, they cried, so that this form of disaster may never occur again! Ironically, many of these prophets whose message centered on reconnection and relationship with God ended up becoming remnants themselves, cut off or even killed for their views.

There always seemed to be a remnant who either remained faithful or returned to being faithful to their covenant relationship with God. These are the ones who, in opposition to the majority who had gone astray, sought to serve God as their faithful ancestors had done. It is through these remnants that the divine character of connection continued to be revealed through humanity. One of the most clearcut historical events showcasing this is the Israelites' return to Jerusalem after seventy years of captivity in Babylon.

In the year 587 or 586 BCE, King Nebuchadnezzar II of Babylon destroyed the city of Jerusalem, including the temple. He took many of the people back with him to Babylon and held them captive there. The last chapter of 2 Chronicles is among the passages that describe not only the fall of Jerusalem at the hands of Nebuchadnezzar, but the perceived reason this devastation occurred: as punishment for their unfaithfulness and breaking their covenant relationship with God.

> All the leading priests and the people also were exceedingly unfaithful, following all the abominations of the nations, and they polluted the house of the Lord that he had consecrated in Jerusalem.
>
> The Lord, the God of their ancestors, sent persistently to them by his messengers, because he had compassion on his people and on his dwelling place, but they kept mocking the messengers of God, despising his words, and scoffing at his prophets until the wrath of the Lord against his people became so great that there was no remedy.
>
> Therefore he brought up against them the king of the Chaldeans, who killed their youths with the sword in the house of their sanctuary and had no compassion on young man or young woman, the aged or the feeble; he gave them all into his hand. All the vessels of the house of God, large and small, and the treasures of the house of the Lord, and the treasures of the king and of his officials, all these he brought to Babylon. They burned the house of God, broke down the wall of Jerusalem, burned all its palaces with fire, and destroyed all its precious vessels. He took into exile in Babylon those who had escaped from the sword, and they became servants to him and to his sons until the establishment of the kingdom of Persia, to fulfill the word of the Lord by the mouth of Jeremiah, until the land had made up for its Sabbaths. All the days that it lay desolate it kept Sabbath, to fulfill seventy years. (2 Chronicles 36:14–21)

It was during much of this time that prophetic voices continued to claim that a remnant would not only survive but would return to Jerusalem and rebuild. This remnant would be charged with reestablishing the covenant and living in faithful relationship to God, keeping God's ways and living again as God's people. And more than fifty years later, in 539 BCE, the Persian army led by King Cyrus overthrew Babylon. Within a year he allowed the captive Israelites to return to their homeland, and many did. The author of the book of Ezra writes,

> In the first year of King Cyrus of Persia, to fulfill the word of the Lord from the mouth of Jeremiah, the Lord stirred up the spirit of King Cyrus of Persia so that he made a proclamation throughout all his kingdom and also in writing, saying: "Thus says King Cyrus of Persia: The Lord, the God of heaven, has given me all the kingdoms of the earth, and he has charged me to build him a house at Jerusalem, which is in Judah. Let any of those among you who are of his people—may their God be with them!—go up to Jerusalem in Judah and rebuild the house of the Lord, the God of Israel; he is the God who is in Jerusalem. (Ezra 1:1–3)

This remnant group returned to Jerusalem and, faithful for the time being, began immediately to rebuild the temple, starting with the altar, so that they could resume worship. This is precisely what a remnant people given a new chance ought to do. Although they soon became distracted and took up other priorities, a smaller version of the temple eventually was completed and life as God's people began again. They were committed to absolute devotion to God's ways and became stricter in their adherence to the law. They believed that would avoid future occurrences of enemy victories. As will unfortunately happen, the interpretation of the law became a struggle for righteousness and the original purpose for all their devotion derailed. The keeping of the law according to those in power became an end unto itself rather than a lifestyle pointing to a relational, covenantal connection to the Divine.

Individuality that separates doesn't always get along with connection that unifies. Yet, as stated previously in this book, if individual gain continues to have cultural rewards, those in power will always search for quicker and more convenient ways to justify those broken ways, in opposition to the nature of God. The Hebrew prophets were not alone in proclaiming the need for a remnant group to reconnect with the Divine.

Islam

Around the end of the sixth century, in what is now Saudi Arabia, a young twenty-five-year-old man named Mohammed received what he believed to be a message from God through the angel Gabriel. Frightened by the radical nature of this revelation, he spoke of this experience only to the people closest to him. Over time, he began to speak more boldly about this message, saying that God was calling humanity to avoid those things that serve only oneself at the expense of others, activities such as debauchery, drunkenness, and cruelty. They were called to turn instead to the will of God in connecting to others through lifting up the weak and helpless, aiding the poor, sacrificing for the sake of justice, and in general serving the greater good. In other words, moving away from isolating behaviors toward connecting, relational behaviors.

As was generally also the case with the prophets in ancient Israel, this message of a single divine nature of connectivity to the rest of humanity was met with protest by those in power. As a metaphor of his message of a single God that unites all things, Mohammed built a single temple where this one Divinity could be worshiped. The contextual point being that any other temple implied the possibility of other gods, or at least other messages from God. This temple was built in the trade town of Mecca, near the coast of the Red Sea, which happened to thrive in the religion business.

At least a hundred temples to different deities existed in Mecca and brought pilgrims to this regional trade center from all over the known world, therefore encouraging at least a hundred different religious rites. As long as these diverse pilgrims were in

Mecca, they may as well purchase a few days of rest from their travels in comfortable accommodations, hang out with some fellow travelers in taverns and purchase some food and drink, buy a few trinkets in shops, and otherwise conduct some business. All this catered to these tourists and profited the business owners. If Mohammed's message of a single God who is all things and connects all things were to catch on, the fear was that varied religious tourists may not feel as welcomed, and the profits from their religious pilgrimages may just disappear too.

Because he defied those seeking to make a profit from religious trade, throughout his life plots of Mohammed's demise were multiple. Yet he somehow escaped them for decades and continued a message of one God whose purpose for humanity is relationship and connectivity. In serving the poor, one is serving God. No one is outside the love and compassion of this single Divinity. That connection to God and others takes priority over profit, power, and prestige.

This minority message was so threatening to those benefitting from the existent system that as the movement grew, the followers of Mohammed found themselves attacked repeatedly—often violently. This resulted in the emphasis of these Muslims shifting from a commitment to empathetic solidarity with the poor to, literally, surviving. Then, in 632 CE, Mohammed himself became sick and died, and the connecting, relational message of this remnant prophet, like virtually all religions before and since, began to turn inward, prioritizing the acquisition and preservation of power over others. Rather than existing as a means of connecting to the poor and victims of injustice, Islam slowly began to be shaped by internal power struggles of authority and strategies of conquest.[3]

The original mission of Islam was connection to a single God and to humanity for the benefit of all. Again, this is the default setting of creation. Like so many other religions, philosophies, and traditions that begin this way, this divinely natural characteristic becomes subverted by doctrines, dogmas, and specifics. Yet, a divine ideology nonetheless survives as a remnant within Islam.

3. Ansary, *Destiny Disrupted*, ch. 2.

Two Contemporary Remnants

The pattern, seen over and over by multiple segments of society in many times and cultures, is to drift away from our default setting into a search for individual betterment, wealth, or power at the expense of empathetic connection. When that (predictably) doesn't work out as planned, things go awry and a remnant again rises with a message that rings true to the natural order of creation, the way of interconnection, empathy, compassion, and love.

Martin Luther King Jr.

The call by the Rev. Dr. Martin Luther King Jr. offers a more recent and powerful example of a remnant of the divine nature of connection pushing back against a cultural majority of separation. Since 1619, when the first African people were kidnapped from their homes and forced into permanent enslavement in this country, there has been a separation between Black and White people that has never closed. Dr. King emphasized the unnaturalness of this partition as a blatant opposition to the ways of a God of justice and unity. In his address given at the "March on Washington for Jobs and Freedom" in Washington, DC on August 28, 1963, he passionately voiced, "Now is the time to make real the promises of democracy. Now is the time to rise from the dark and desolate valley of segregation to the sunlit path of racial justice. Now is the time to lift our nation from the quick sands of racial injustice to the solid rock of brotherhood. Now is the time to make justice a reality for all of God's children."[4]

His work and passion were foundational to the Civil Rights Movement of the 1950s and 60s. As a result, social justice and equality for Black Americans took significant strides forward. Segregation became illegal in public places, it ended discrimination against immigrants based on the region from which they originated, and it provided the right to vote for people of color and the elimination of barriers to voting.

4. King, "I Have a Dream," para. 7.

His impassioned message of equality resulted in his assassination on April 4, 1968, on the balcony outside his room at the Lorraine Motel in Memphis, Tennessee. Again, individuality that separates often conflicts with connection that unifies. Unity, equality, and justice for all people, even though these are the ways of nature, the universe, and the Divine, generally emerge as a remnant ideology in opposition to a majority view. Sadly, much of Dr. King's work and the work of this remnant movement is, at least for now, being turned back in many parts of the country.

Mahatma Gandhi

Mahatma Mohandas Karamchand Gandhi provides another testimony of a remnant movement toward compassion and justice. A lawyer, politician, and social activist, he led a struggle for India's independence from British rule that, although controversial, became successful in 1947.

Unable to establish a law practice in India upon passing the bar in Britain, Gandhi moved to South Africa to begin practicing law. He initially was not interested in politics. This changed, however, after he experienced firsthand violent discrimination, such as being thrown off a train by a White train official because of his skin color. After several such incidents with Whites in South Africa, Gandhi's thinking and focus changed, and he felt he must stand up for those who experienced segregation and separation. He insisted that violence was not a way to achieve unity and justice, so he practiced a remnant philosophy of nonviolence throughout his life. He entered politics to put an end to the violent segregation in South Africa and India.

In 1915, at age forty-five, he returned to India and soon set about organizing peasants, farmers, and urban laborers to protest excessive land tax and discrimination. Assuming leadership of the Indian National Congress in 1921, Gandhi led nationwide campaigns for easing poverty, expanding women's rights, building religious and ethnic amity, ending untouchability, and, above all, achieving the people's self-rule. Gandhi adopted the short dhoti woven with hand-spun yarn as a mark of identification with and connection to India's rural poor. He began to live in a self-sufficient residential community, to eat simple food, and undertake long fasts as a means of both introspection and political protest.

Gandhi's vision of an independent India based on religious pluralism, equality, and the worth of every person was challenged in the early 1940s by a Muslim nationalism movement that demanded a separate homeland for Muslims within British India. In August 1947, Britain granted independence, but the British Indian Empire was partitioned into two dominions, a Hindu-majority India and a Muslim-majority Pakistan. As many of the displaced Hindus, Muslims, and Sikhs made their way to their new lands, religious violence broke out. In the months that followed, Gandhi went on several hunger strikes to stop the religious violence. The last of these, in January of 1948, when he was seventy-eight, led to the belief by some that Gandhi had been too tolerant of both Pakistani and Indian Muslims. Among these was Nathuram Godse, a militant Hindu nationalist, who assassinated Gandhi by firing three bullets into his chest while on his way to an interfaith prayer meeting in Delhi on January 30, 1948.[5]

Again, individuality that separates doesn't always get along with connection that unifies. Unity, equality, and justice for all people, even though these are the ways of nature, the universe, and the Divine, generally emerge as a remnant ideology in opposition to a majority view. Gandhi was killed instantly.

The Early Church

The crucifixion of Jesus of Nazareth was largely motivated by the same cultural forces that brought about the assassinations of King and Gandhi. As long as individual gain continues to have cultural rewards, those in power will always seek to eliminate anything that threatens that sense of separation and superiority, even to the

---

5. Cush et al., *Encyclopedia of Hinduism*, 544.

point of killing. They will justify those broken ways though they are in direct opposition to God.

Following the death of Jesus, his followers were in a quandary as to what would happen next. They huddled in fear, partially because they assumed the authorities would bestow upon them the same penalty they gave Jesus. Beyond that, with their leader gone they felt completely unqualified to carry on in his name. They weren't even sure if carrying on was a good idea.

The reported sightings of a risen Christ a few days later gave them hope that this compassionate, merciful mission of God could continue. But not long afterward they spoke of his ascension into heaven, leaving them frustrated, frightened, and alone once more.

The day of Pentecost as recorded in the second chapter of the book of Acts turned the tables. These disciples "were filled with the Holy Spirit and began to speak in other languages, as the Spirit gave them ability" (Acts 2:4). According to Acts, they changed from being a helpless band to a determined remnant, ready to reveal the nature of God as they experienced it in Jesus. That became their focus and their purpose. The book of Acts records them healing the sick, challenging the separatist elites, and feeding the hungry. In all manner of things, they were lifting up those who were left behind, left out, or otherwise had no place at the table. Jesus had been the embodiment of this unifying nature of God, and now they felt equipped to continue that mission. No one was outside the connection of God, even the Gentiles. In that way they carried Jesus' work even further than he himself did. All are loved, all are included, all are equal, all are to be shown mercy. All are connected to each other and to the Divine. This was the reason the first disciples of Jesus organized into what later became a "church." It all had to do with compassion, care, and unity in Jesus' name. This little remnant group of Jesus-followers was surprisingly effective. For decades they faced persecution, imprisonment, and even death from the majority power (Rome) without significant wavering.

They held on to that mission for quite a while—about three centuries, in fact. But then, as always seems to happen, the search

CONNECTED

for power at the expense of others derailed the remnant movement.
Once Emperor Constantine of Rome issued the Edict of Milan in
313 CE, legalizing Christianity, it lost its remnant status and became partner to the state. Not too long after, in 380 CE, Emperor
Theodosius signed the Edict of Thessalonica, making Christianity
the official religion of the state, which confirmed and solidified the
influence of Christianity not only on the Roman world at the time
but also for the rest of world history. Theodosius was also the last
emperor to rule before Rome was split between West and East for
the first time, meaning his legalization reached all territories.[6]

This resulted in Christianity becoming inseparable from
the empire, able to use and to justify the same violent, powerful,
militaristic methods that have been used throughout history by
conquerors. For the first time, however, this was being done in
the name of Jesus the Christ, the chosen one of God. As long
as individual gain continues to have cultural rewards, those in
power will always seek to eliminate anything that threatens that
sense of separation and superiority, even to the point of killing.
They will justify those broken ways though they are in direct
opposition to God. Even the church. And despite some sincere
efforts, we've never fully recovered.

The point of this chapter is that history has multiple examples
of the connective default setting of creation, this image of God,
arising anew in defiant remnants. Therein lies the hope of the
church. There may be some remnants of the character of the Divine emerging among us. That is the subject of the next chapter.

For Discussion

1. How does the idea of a small, surviving remnant challenge
   the generally accepted thinking that in most ways, "bigger
   is better"?

2. Most congregations are shrinking in members. Many will
   close within the next several years. What will you do if

6. Wade, "Rome's Conversion," paras. 4, 8.

the faith community you attend (if you attend) is one that doesn't survive?

3. This chapter asserts that there will always be a remnant of the church present and revealing the divine image of connection. What do you think it takes to be part of that remnant? To be part of that remnant, what changes need to happen in your community of faith?

4. Most of Christian history shows the church aligned with the state. The result has been a version of Christianity that readily uses the state's methods of power, status, and authority to separate itself from the rest of the world and acquire its own desired ends. Do you believe such a version of the church ought to survive? Why or why not?

CHAPTER 7

Hope

Hopelessness

IN THE INTRODUCTION TO this book, I mentioned that I had resigned as a member of the clergy of the Evangelical Lutheran Church in America (ELCA) amidst a sense of hopelessness. My denomination is certainly no worse than any other, but it is nonetheless part of a general Christian derailment that includes virtually the entirety of the church. At that point I had devoted more than thirty-five years to this pastoral endeavor, and although those years included growth in the areas of church membership, Sunday morning worship attendance, and financial giving in the congregations I had served,[1] I considered myself a miserable failure. Most of the growth was, quite honestly, due to people's personal dissatisfaction with a previous congregation resulting in a transfer of membership from their church to mine. I'm a good storyteller, so my sermons were relatively easy to listen to. When combined with a policy of "all are invited" to the Communion table, people usually felt included. I emphasized hospitality

---

1. The trifecta of perceived church success, which makes it part of the problem.

to visitors on Sunday mornings, so most people felt comfortable and welcomed in my congregations.

But nothing of any significance ever changed. I was unable to help any congregation genuinely recognize that the church is about connection with those outside the church, those impoverished, oppressed, and pushed aside, much less commit to that purpose. I was seen as successful by some because numbers increased—hardly the model Jesus embodied or proclaimed. It seemed that when an opportunity came for us to step into a deeper connection with those who were outside of the church, the discomfort of doing so won the day. I remember one particular incident that revealed this to me in no uncertain terms.

The church I was serving at the time had spent considerable effort and energy articulating their purpose, why they existed in that neighborhood. We discerned together that their primary reason for being there was to connect more directly to the church's neighborhood and be a relational presence of unconditional love, inclusion, and advocacy for those often left behind. This took a long time, was discerned together as a whole congregation, and reflected something it seemed Jesus would affirm. I took this as a sign of movement toward the divine purpose of the church. This purpose, or mission, was lifted up, celebrated, and spoken of frequently throughout the congregation. What followed were fairly well attended studies on racism, poverty, and gender identity. A majority seemed to be on board.

One afternoon a few months later, I received a call from a colleague who was affiliated with the Black Lives Matter movement. Their neighborhood group (which was very near our church building) had been gathering once a week on a street corner to hold signs of support for African Americans and the injustice they far too often receive. My colleague told me that their usual corner was unavailable that night and asked if I would allow their group to park in our church parking lot so they could gather on the four corners of the intersection near our church. Since this was an opportunity to actually connect with our immediate neighbors in support of people who had been victims of centuries of injustice, and since no other activities were planned at the church that evening, I consented. After all, the congregation had recently said that they existed exactly for things like this. A few hours later, about fifteen cars pulled into our parking lot and a quiet group gathered at the intersection, holding signs affirming that, indeed, Black lives do matter.

I received a phone call a day or two later from an incensed church member saying that I had crossed a line. I was putting the church at risk because of the violence associated with these protests, also indicating our church should not be taking political stands. Plus, they added, there was an insurance hazard if someone were to fall in our parking lot and injure themselves.

The executive committee met secretly, resulting in a decision to censure me, insisting that I never make those kinds of decisions again. Although I pointed out that the congregation had previously committed to connecting with our neighborhood for the sake of those marginalized, the argument was ignored. My perceived indiscretion was then brought to the entirety of the church council, who, after a long and passionate discussion, did end up supporting my decision by a slim majority and said there was ultimately no need to refer me to the bishop or censure me further.

But the damage had been done. After many years of consistent service in that congregation, I was thereafter publicly called out as untrustworthy. Rather than being the pastor who lived out the very purpose the congregation itself had discerned, approved, and celebrated, I was now looked upon with suspicion and became a scapegoat for any congregational difficulty, real or imagined. This was further evidence to me that significant change appeared hopeless. Reflecting the image of God was difficult enough to talk about in the church but was hopelessly impossible to live.

This was but one of multiple instances I experienced throughout years of congregational service. There always seemed to be resistance to seriously considering any significant redirection. Rather than continuing to beat my head against a brick wall, I felt resignation was my best option. Which I did. I searched for other employment but my resume, which included the postgraduate degrees of Master of Divinity and Doctor of Ministry, as well as many years of working as a pastor, was, according to a consultant, "too churchy." I finally ended up working for a time in a university bookstore. As it turned out, I had several significant conversations with fellow bookstore employees, who, when they eventually discovered my previous vocation, asked wonderfully pointed questions. Many revealed to me the pain they had experienced at the hands of the church. Some student employees explained why they had quit their parents' church, related how they felt the church was unhelpful or irrelevant to their life journey, or described their own faith story and how Christianity felt too exclusive for them. So many of these conversations were like others I have had with people outside the church over the years.

A while later I received a call from the bishop's office, wondering if I would consider taking on an "Intentional Interim" pastoral position in a neighboring state. To his credit, the bishop patiently waited until I quit laughing, and then told me that I ought to consider it because it seemed to fit my passion and style.

In my denomination, Intentional Interim Ministry happens when a congregation's pastor resigns or retires. Since the loss of a pastor and the call of a new one means, by definition, there will be significant change in the life of a congregation, often a trained interim pastor will be sent there to facilitate that change from what has been to what could be. It offered, he informed me, the opportunity to step into a congregation that already knows change is coming and may be open to reexamining other types of change as well. The church needs to change, he said, and that which I had been espousing for years may be a helpful step for congregations to make should they choose to take it.

Partly because it did sound a little interesting and partly because finding other significant employment was proving difficult, I eventually accepted this opportunity. I enrolled in the required interim pastor training course and took a position at a church in a university city close to the Mexican border in a nearby state. Still filled with doubt as to the future of the church and my role in it, I set out to listen in this new church, to discover how (or if) they may be open to a deeper examination of their purpose, and converse with them about what that might look like for them. To my delight, not only did this congregation recognize that the future of their congregation must look different from their past, but they were also enthusiastic about it. They desired change. They were passionate about connecting more significantly with their neighborhood, which included a high number of refugees, immigrants, and impoverished people as well as university students and faculty. I found myself edging ever-so-slightly away from hopelessness toward hope.

It occurred to me later that this slow movement from hopelessness to hope is also part of the divine image. This hope connects us to the possibilities and to what that connection can look like. This hope renews us in a divine purpose and offers a new way of living into that purpose. Perhaps that is what the original disciples of Jesus experienced on Easter.

Resurrection

At the death of Jesus all was lost for his disciples; all hope was gone. The one to whom they had devoted themselves had been brutally and maliciously killed. Crucifixion, the favored form of capital punishment used by the Roman government, was a long and tortuous process whereby the victim suffered for hours or even days, finally succumbing to asphyxiation when they had no strength left to pull themselves up to breath. For his disciples, it didn't matter now that the charges brought against Jesus were false or that he didn't defend himself against them. He was dead. And the hope he brought with him—that the mercy, love, compassion, and grace of God were just as much for the outcast and the stranger as for the rich and influential—died with him. For them, Jesus was the embodiment of those divine characteristics; he revealed the default setting of divine connection to all people.

Later, church authorities would declare Jesus to be divine himself, thus saying clearly and thoroughly that Jesus was revealing God's will and God's nature for creation. Rather than using division and tribalism to strengthen Jewish views against the Romans and the Samaritans, or followers of the Pharisees against followers of the Sadducees, Jesus revealed the divine order of the kingdom of God for all. Keith Giles writes in a *Patheos* blog post,

> The ideas Jesus introduced in the first three Synoptic Gospels about the Kingdom of God being within us eventually led to the even more startling statements found in the Gospel of John where Jesus says:
>
> > *"In that day you will know that I am in my Father, and you in me, and I in you."* [John 14:20]
>
> This radical idea that Jesus realizes that he is in God and that we are in him and he is in us is probably one of the most anti-division statements found in the entire New Testament.
>
> It's an idea that, if it were to spread to everyone, might lead to the end of Religion as we know it, and the downfall of Empires everywhere.
>
> Because if everyone is already in God's Kingdom, we don't need religious systems to experience it.
>
> Because if everyone is as connected to one another as we are to God, then how could we ever go to war and kill someone who is essentially connected to ourselves and to the Divine?
>
> The concept of Division is one that Jesus strongly denied. It's why he told us to love our enemies. It's why he emphasized the importance of forgiveness. It's why he taught us to pray a prayer of community where we cared about everyone and not just ourselves.[2]

Now all that hope for the kingdom of God present among them was gone. These disciples understandably knew that without Jesus, they had neither the skills nor the will to continue his mission in the world. The power of Rome was too oppressive and the religious power around them was too absolute. There was no hope of anything changing. If Jesus couldn't do it, these lowly disciples had no chance whatsoever. It was hopeless.

---

2. Giles, "Why the World," paras. 9–15.

Yet a couple of days after the death of Jesus, they found themselves edging away from hopelessness toward hope. The gospel of Mark describes the beginning of this fledgling movement out of hopelessness as follows:

> When the Sabbath was over, Mary Magdalene and Mary the mother of James and Salome bought spices, so that they might go and anoint him. And very early on the first day of the week, when the sun had risen, they went to the tomb. They had been saying to one another, "Who will roll away the stone for us from the entrance to the tomb?" When they looked up, they saw that the stone, which was very large, had already been rolled back. As they entered the tomb, they saw a young man dressed in a white robe sitting on the right side, and they were alarmed. But he said to them, "Do not be alarmed; you are looking for Jesus of Nazareth, who was crucified. He has been raised; he is not here. Look, there is the place they laid him. But go, tell his disciples and Peter that he is going ahead of you to Galilee; there you will see him, just as he told you." So they went out and fled from the tomb, for terror and amazement had seized them, and they said nothing to anyone, for they were afraid. (Mark 16:1–8)

I find it helpful that this original ending to the Gospel of Mark[3] indicates that these early disciples were too terrified to talk about what they had seen and heard. The resurrection of Jesus was preposterous, and they were already being watched by authorities due to their association with Jesus. But this unlikely story offered something they hadn't had since his death: hope. If nothing else, the stories of Jesus being raised from the dead should offer us that. According to some of the earliest biblical authors, that which seems impossible perhaps shouldn't be immediately written off as such. Regardless of how one interprets these Gospel narratives, I believe they give us some wiggle room to hope. Hope for the world, and even for the church.

---

3. Our current Bible contains two additional endings to Mark, usually referred to as the "shorter ending" and the "longer ending," both of which were added later.

Hope

What follows are just a few examples of congregations or ministries that seem to have grasped some measure of resurrection hope. I include them not as an exhaustive list or a prescriptive model for the church, but as a small spark of resurrection, of the divine image of imaginative connection that can be revealed through the church. These ministries, against all odds, are a remnant sampling of some who have found creative and new ways to connect to God by going all-in to be in relationship with their broader community in love, compassion, empathy, and grace. In other words, they reveal the image of God exhibited by all of creation. And they do so in ways that the church was initially called and committed to do in keeping with the life, ministry, and teachings of Jesus. Some of these are not well received by the institutional church. Others have the larger church's blessing. It's an interesting mix.

Wholly Kicks

Founded by former pastor Tyg Taylor, this 501(c)(3) ministry recently was started as an imaginative way to meet a particular need present in the Denver metropolitan area. Working with hundreds of volunteers and partnering with numerous other non-profits, Wholly Kicks exists to provide shoes and socks for any who are economically distressed, among the most requested items by the unhoused population, refugees, and those seeking asylum. Wholly Kicks operates with the value that all people, regardless of circumstances, background, or journey, are worthy of dignity and love. According to Taylor,

> We love people by providing dignity, respect, kindness and the need of shoes that just eases the economic burden. We witness to other nonprofits how to work side by side with neighbors and friends, instead of offering products from behind a table. We get down on our knees and hold the feet of folks of all ages from all parts of the world (right in our community). We set people in motion for

a common vision that we believe everyone is a Whole person (no pecking order or brokenness we need to fix).

Wholly Kicks begins with the assumption that everyone is worthwhile and everyone matters, regardless of life circumstances, economic status, legal documentation, or housing condition. Rather than offering forgiveness to the repentant, they offer shoes to any in need. Instead of doctrines to draw one closer to God, they offer dignity and worth in the image of God. Wholly Kicks consistently shares stories of transformation and love through a direct connection with those who, quite simply, need shoes.

It seems relatively simple to provide shoes to the shoeless, connecting with them on a level of dignity and value in the image of God. Though some congregations may be involved in serving ministries akin to this as a sideline or an afterthought, the people at Wholly Kicks die to themselves and their institutional survival to meet this most basic need. For most churches, this level of connection with their surrounding community gets lost amid self-preservation and the maintenance of traditions. Wholly Kicks has abandoned virtually all traditional church trappings to fully embrace the path and teachings of Jesus.

Not only does this ministry emphatically connect with those receiving "kicks," but also with its hundreds of volunteers who share that vision of connection and worth. Beyond that, donors are an integral part of the interconnected system that offers footwear to those without it. The divine image of God is revealed through these deeply interwoven connections based on a core belief in all people's innate value, in being worthy of respect, and in being loved by God unconditionally. Deliberately following in the way of Jesus, this ministry offers connections beyond autonomous serving or homogenous friendships and moves beyond separations that are contrary to the divine image. Again, from Taylor:

> I believe that Jesus just walked around, saw stuff, and did something about it. My things with the church have been surrendered to just get good shit done with our neighbors. I believe less needs to be said "to" and more asked "about." Like, "How are you loving the world?

How is God working through your right now? Give a recent story?" I never did believe liturgy was the work of the people, but that the work of the people is actually the work of the people!"

Though technically not a church by many people's definition, Wholly Kicks is a ministry that is completely dedicated to following the life, ministry, and teachings of Jesus. In a very tangible way, they show to any in need a divine connection in the image of God. For more information or to connect with Wholly Kicks, check them out at https://whollykicks.org.

Faith Church

Although Wholly Kicks has found it more effective to connect with God and their community by walking alongside the organized church rather than working from within it, Faith Church in Golden, Colorado takes a different approach, though based on similar values.

Led by Pastor Jane Jebsen, Faith understands their purpose is simply to love God and love others. All else comes from that core belief. More than words, this congregation has evolved in some significant ways over the years to take up this straightforward focus.

For Pastor Jane, the institutional church doesn't necessarily help this congregation meet its calling. She sees denominations as helpful in accomplishing some larger things that individual congregations can't do alone, but isn't sure these official structures can—or should—survive. Jebsen says, "There will always be more and more denominations and denominations within denominations, because as humans we are always going to disagree with someone." Though much of the larger church is intended to reflect the image of the Divine, she suggests that denominations, at a more elementary level, promote separation and division. She acknowledges that the lines between denominations are already growing fainter and that the church is going to have to come to grips with this reality. "What I am hearing from younger folks is the idea of authentic community that does life together and wrestles with the things of faith together. This is very different than showing up in an auditorium, watching what happens on stage, and then leaving."

The people at Faith have adopted three "pillars" that define their existence, guide their decisions, and focus their energy and resources. According Jebsen, "These foundations remind us we are to be constantly growing, seeking, and going out into the world— they help us balance the inward and the outward focus. Helping us ask the important questions like why are we doing this?"

These pillars state that Faith exists to "connect people to authentic community, deepen people's relationship with Jesus, and prepare people for the mission God is calling them into." The creation of small groups that are grounded in practices that deepen authentic connection together is one significant way Faith has chosen to live in the divine image. For the people at Faith, these groups go well beyond Bible studies and friendships. They are set up to be close communities where one can bring all of who they are and still be accepted and encouraged to let others walk with them. In these intentional communities, questions can be safely raised, doubts voiced, and troubles shared.

The core value that everyone is integral, beloved, and equipped takes a deeper meaning in this congregation. Here they utilize some of the traditions and practices of the historic church to support them in their mission. Gathering in worship on Sunday around Scripture and Communion, preaching, and Bible studies are important at Faith. They must, however, relate to everyday life, challenging the congregation to live their faith and their mission in their daily lives. For the people at Faith, that means being "the hands, feet, and voice of Jesus in the world today," driving them into a deeper connection with the broader community. Their vision of this relationship carries them beyond the walls of the church building to connect with households that may never set foot on the church's property. Their core value of loving God and loving others compels them to pay less attention to their own congregational comfort, not fearing the changes necessary to follow Jesus wherever the Spirit leads. Jebsen states,

This is scary and exciting and nerve racking and some days I still want to just walk away—because people are weird—and can be mean and self-centered and afraid and grieving and a thousand other different things. I don't know how much change I will be able to affect, but I can at least affect the part of the world I have some leadership in.

Faith Church lives with the reality that change is necessary, constant, and faithful. They know that the church of tomorrow will look and act differently than it has in the past. Most participants in this congregation understand that they should always be reforming and reshaping in ways that help people—all people—connect their heart to the heart of God. This is evidenced in a recent decision by this congregation to focus on connecting primarily to families with children ages preschool through fifth grade for the next several years. For Faith, this isn't a self-centered church growth strategy, but a prayerfully discerned means to build relationships in one underserved demographic around them. The goal is to connect and serve this part of their surrounding community rather than increase their own numbers. To accomplish this, they have committed themselves to reform the congregation in any way necessary to support this task. Their vision for this states, "Imagine you're a family with kids ages preschool through fifth grade trying to navigate life, who potentially feels isolated, overwhelmed, and disconnected. Then imagine a community that is waiting to embrace your whole family, walking alongside you in all aspects of life: emotional, social, financial, spiritual."

Instead of wanting young families to join their church for the benefit of the church, Faith is envisioning a connection with young families in meeting the needs of those families. And they are willing to change, adapt, evolve, and risk losing current members to reveal this image of God to do it. For more information on Faith, find them at https://faithgolden.org.

Lakewood Connects

Not far from Faith Church in Golden, Colorado is the city of Lakewood. This is the home of a unique ministry called Lakewood Connects. Organized by Reg Cox, who describes himself as the "community connector/organizer, communicator, and navigator," Lakewood Connects exists to reduce suffering in their city by building effective service partnerships between church, government, education, and business.

This imaginative ministry began in 2005 with a small group of eight pastors gathering monthly for prayer and support. To better understand and therefore serve their surrounding community, they began to invite various business, government, and educational leaders from the community to a quarterly lunch for the purpose of listening and learning. At one of these luncheons, the Lakewood Police chief met with this group of pastors and indicated that some significant needs were being seen in some local elementary schools. These needs included families dealing with food insecurity, a lack of school resources, and dropping enrollment due to more affluent families moving their children to more affluent schools. He encouraged this group of pastors to connect with and serve these elementary schools if they wanted to make a difference in the city. Soon thereafter the mayor and city council were invited to join this group of pastors to hear directly from school principals about the seriousness of their families' needs and how they could best serve at-risk schools. Too many schools were struggling with a rising "free and reduced lunch" population, low academic scores, high discipline issues, low enrollment, and low staff morale. The meeting spurred church and city officials to create a partnership between churches, community organizations, and city leaders to find assets together that could be utilized for these least-resourced schools and the families most impacted by them.

One of the first cooperative and successful projects involved transforming a derelict portion of one Title 1 elementary school's property into a state-of-the-art soccer field, available not only to the school but to the entire community. Labeled the "Field of

Dreams" project, this coalition of churches, businesses, city government, and schools raised $500,000 to renovate the outdoor play field. This was so successful that similar partnerships were created to raise $400,000 to renovate two other schools.

Community Connector Reg Cox believes the purpose of the church as the body of Christ is to fulfill the mission of Jesus, offering a connection to God for all humanity. That reunification "offers a greater sense of meaning and purpose than the usual self-fulfillment pursuits natural to humanity." The church can certainly include corporate gatherings for worship, he says, but the emphasis must always be on community connection and relationship-building beyond its own walls. According to Cox, too many churches exist for their own sake, prioritizing their "edifice and monument making." Lakewood Connects therefore promotes "church different," meaning, among other things, that the church exists to "support their local community; find ways to reduce suffering; convene resources and goodwill to reduce suffering in the city; collaborate with unlikely partners; and build proactive partnerships with government, education, business, and all faith communities to reduce suffering." Lakewood Connects understands that the "sanctuary model" of church may be ending. This awareness has spurred them to sponsor imaginative conversations in the community around church buildings being transformed into community centers where anyone can walk in and find answers, solutions, or accompaniment to their life struggles. Otherwise, says Cox, "what good is church?" To find out more about Lakewood Connects, visit them at https://lakewoodconnects.org.

Again, these examples are but a few of the remnant faith communities seeking to reveal a divine connection within their contexts. They can offer a glimpse of hope that the default setting of creation, i.e., connection to all, deliberate empathy, unconditional love, and profound compassion, can still be exhibited through the church for the sake of the world. May it be so.

For Discussion

1. Many people have given up on the church, believing it to be (among other things) an archaic, disconnected, judgmental, out-of-touch, hypocritical institution that does more harm than good. If you are still part of the church, why do you continue? If not, why not?

2. This chapter includes a few examples of different expressions of church that have made significant changes to connect with their surrounding contexts in divine ways. What other examples are you aware of? Do they provide any hope for you? If so, how?

3. Do you agree that there is hope that the church can regain its purpose of divine connection in the world? How will you contribute to that hope of connection, mutuality, and reciprocity in your own context?

4. If you were to find a church, congregation, or spiritual community that, in the manner revealed by Jesus, made authentic connection, empathy, and love a higher priority than doctrine, ritual, and self-preservation, how likely would you be to give it a try? Why or why not?

APPENDIX

A Study on Values, Mission, and Vision

IF YOU SO CHOOSE, a brief Bible study is included here. Participation in this four-session Bible study on portions of the book of Acts can help a congregation gain a fuller understanding of its identity and purpose through articulating its values, mission, and vision. The more people who join this Bible study series, the more clarity there will be as to how to discover and articulate the values, mission, and vision that allow the congregation to acknowledge their identity. Out of this identity, the congregation can discern its purpose and more accurately plan, make decisions, and move into the future according to their giftedness and passions.

Session 1: The Apostles Are Persecuted

Acts 5:25–32

Then someone arrived and announced, "Look, the men whom you put in prison are standing in the temple and teaching the people!" Then the captain went with the temple police and brought them, but without violence, for they were afraid of being stoned by the people.

When they had brought them, they had them stand before the council. The high priest questioned them, saying, "We gave you strict orders not to teach in this name, yet here you have filled Jerusalem with your teaching and you are determined to bring this man's blood on us." But Peter and the apostles answered, "We must obey God rather than any human authority. The God of our ancestors raised up Jesus, whom you had killed by hanging him on a tree. God exalted him at his right hand as Leader and Savior that he might give repentance to Israel and forgiveness of sins. And we are witnesses to these things, and so is the Holy Spirit whom God has given to those who obey him."

Core Values

1. This is now the third time the apostles have been arrested for teaching about Jesus' death and resurrection. What values do they hold that are guiding their decision to continue this activity even though it means risking arrest?

2. To get a better grasp on the role of core values, consider the following: if the apostles had chosen to stop teaching, thereby avoiding arrest, what values could have been guiding that decision? Are these core values different than those they exhibited in the text?

3. The council in Jerusalem had decided to reprimand the apostles again. What values do they hold that guided this decision?

4. Consider a difficult decision you've had to make. Can you identify the core values behind your choice? How did it work out?

5. Have your core values changed over the course of your lifetime? If so, how?

Mission

1. What is the purpose (mission) of these apostles as they continue to teach about Jesus? What are they trying to accomplish? What would you say is their "measure of success"?

2. Which verse(s) in this text best articulate the apostles' mission at this point?

3. The mission of the temple police and the council is certainly different than that of the apostles. What is their goal? What is their measure of success?

4. Which verse(s) in this text best articulate the high priest/council's mission?

5. Have you thought about whether you have a mission/purpose? If so, what is it? Has it changed?

Vision

1. If the apostles are wildly successful in their mission, what would that look like (what would the vision be)? What would be different?

2. If the council is wildly successful in their mission, what would that look like?

3. Are visions ever attainable? Should they be?

4. Begin to think about a vision for your congregation. How would you know if this aligns with the divine nature?

Session 2: The Transformation of Saul

Acts 9:1–19a

Saul, still breathing threats and murder against the disciples of the Lord, went to the high priest and asked him for letters to the synagogues at Damascus, so that if he found any who belonged to the Way, men or women, he might bring them bound to Jerusalem. Now as he was going along and approaching Damascus, suddenly a light from heaven flashed around him. He fell to the ground and heard a voice saying to him, "Saul, Saul, why do you persecute me?" He asked, "Who are you, Lord?" The reply came, "I am Jesus, whom you are persecuting. But get up and enter the city, and you will be told what you are to do." The men who were traveling with him stood speechless because they heard the voice but saw no one. Saul got up from the ground, and though his eyes were open, he could see nothing; so they led him by the hand and brought him into Damascus. For three days he was without sight, and neither ate nor drank.

Now there was a disciple in Damascus named Ananias. The Lord said to him in a vision, "Ananias." He answered, "Here I am, Lord." The Lord said to him, "Get up and go to the street called Straight, and at the house of Judas look for a man of Tarsus named Saul. At this moment he is praying, and he has seen in a vision a man named Ananias come in and lay his hands on him so that he might regain his sight." But Ananias answered, "Lord, I have heard from many about this man, how much evil he has done to your saints in Jerusalem; and here he has authority from the chief priests to bind all who invoke your name." But the Lord said to him, "Go, for he is an instrument whom I have chosen to bring my name before Gentiles and kings and before the people of Israel; I myself will show him how much he must suffer for the sake of my name." So Ananias went and entered the house. He laid his hands on Saul and said, "Brother Saul, the Lord Jesus, who appeared to you on your way here, has sent me so that you may regain your sight and be filled with the Holy Spirit." And immediately something like scales fell from his eyes, and his sight was restored. Then he got up and was baptized, and after taking some food, he regained his strength.

Core Values

1. How do you think Saul could justify persecution of those who follow Jesus? What values guided that?

2. Imagine being in the place of Ananias. Why does he resist the direction from the Lord to go to Saul? What values are revealed in his hesitancy?

3. Do you believe Saul's values changed after his encounter with the risen Jesus? If so, how are they different? If not, how are they lived out in such divergent ways?

4. Think of a time when your own core values have been challenged. What was going on? How did your values guide you? Did your values change?

Mission

1. What was Saul's mission prior to (and in the first verses of) this text?

2. Do you think Saul believed he was serving God in his persecution of the church? If so, how would he justify persecution? If not, what would he be serving?

3. Saul's mission obviously took a dramatic turn. What is his mission by the end of this text?

4. Can your congregation have a mission apart from the risen Jesus? If not, why not? If so, how?

Vision

1. What would have been Saul's vision had he been able to complete his initial mission?

2. Can you articulate the vision for his new, altered mission?

3. How do you understand God's role in the renewed vision?

4. Would God's role be similar in a vision for your congregation? How?

Session 3: Philip and the Ethiopian Eunuch

Acts 8:26–40

Then an angel of the Lord said to Philip, "Get up and go toward the south to the road that goes down from Jerusalem to Gaza." (This is a wilderness road.) So he got up and went. Now there was an Ethiopian eunuch, a court official of the Candace, queen of the Ethiopians, in charge of her entire treasury. He had come to Jerusalem to worship and was returning home; seated in his chariot, he was reading the prophet Isaiah. Then the Spirit said to Philip, "Go over to this chariot and join it." So Philip ran up to it and heard him reading the prophet Isaiah. He asked, "Do you understand what you are reading?" He replied, "How can I, unless someone guides me?" And he invited Philip to get in and sit beside him. Now the passage of the scripture that he was reading was this:

"Like a sheep he was led to the slaughter, and like a lamb silent before its shearer, so he does not open his mouth. In his humiliation justice was denied him. Who can describe his generation? For his life is taken away from the earth."

The eunuch asked Philip, "About whom, may I ask you, does the prophet say this, about himself or about someone else?" Then Philip began to speak, and starting with this scripture, he proclaimed to him the good news about Jesus. As they were going along the road, they came to some water; and the eunuch said, "Look, here is water! What is to prevent me from being baptized?" He commanded the chariot to stop, and both of them, Philip and the eunuch, went down into the water, and Philip baptized him. When they came up out of the water, the Spirit of the Lord snatched Philip away; the eunuch saw him no more, and went on his way rejoicing. 40 But Philip found himself at Azotus, and as he was passing

through the region, he proclaimed the good news to all
the towns until he came to Caesarea.

Core Values

1. Consider each of the decisions that both Philip and the Ethiopian official made in this text.

2. Why do you think each person made the decisions they made (their core values)?

3. Why do you suppose Philip was open to going up to the Ethiopian's chariot in the first place?

4. What does all this say about the values to which Philip adheres? The Ethiopian official?

5. How are your values like Philip's? How are they like the Ethiopian official's? How are they different?

Mission

1. What was Philip's mission or objective?

2. Did he accomplish that mission? How do you know?

3. What was the Ethiopian eunuch's mission or objective?

4. Was Philip's purpose in this situation the same as God's, do you think? Why do you think that?

5. Do you believe you understand a divine purpose for you? Why or why not?

6. What would help you gain clarity around God's purpose for you?

Vision

1. What does this story reveal about God's vision?

2. How is Philip's mission in this text part of God's larger vision?

3. Do you think the Ethiopian's response is part of God's larger vision? If so, how? If not, why not?

4. Has your vision for God's call to you been expanded by your time with this text? If so, how?

5. Has your vision for what God is calling you into been expanded by this text? If so, how?

Session 4: Peter's Report to the Church at Jerusalem

Acts 11:1–18

Now the apostles and the believers who were in Judea heard that the Gentiles had also accepted the word of God. So when Peter went up to Jerusalem, the circumcised believers criticized him, saying, "Why did you go to uncircumcised men and eat with them?" Then Peter began to explain it to them, step by step, saying, "I was in the city of Joppa praying, and in a trance I saw a vision. There was something like a large sheet coming down from heaven, being lowered by its four corners; and it came close to me. As I looked at it closely I saw four-footed animals, beasts of prey, reptiles, and birds of the air. I also heard a voice saying to me, 'Get up, Peter; kill and eat.' But I replied, 'By no means, Lord; for nothing profane or unclean has ever entered my mouth.' But a second time the voice answered from heaven, 'What God has made clean, you must not call profane.' This happened three times; then everything was pulled up again to heaven. At that very moment three men, sent to me from Caesarea, arrived at the house where we were. The Spirit told me to go with them and not to make a distinction between them and us. These six brothers also accompanied me, and we entered the man's house. He told us how he had seen the angel standing in his house and saying, 'Send to Joppa and bring Simon, who is called Peter; he will give you a message by which you and your entire household will be saved.' And as I began to speak, the Holy Spirit fell upon them just as it had upon us at the beginning. And I remembered the word of the Lord, how he had said, 'John baptized with water, but you will be baptized with the Holy Spirit.' If then God gave them the same gift that he gave us when we believed in the Lord Jesus Christ, who was I that I could hinder God?" When they heard this, they were silenced. And they praised God, saying, "Then God has given even to the Gentiles the repentance that leads to life."

Core Values

1. What values were guiding Peter's initial decision to decline the voice's command to kill and eat the "unclean animals" (v. 8)?

2. Peter eventually changed his mind. Did his core values change? If so, how? If not, how was he living the same values in such a different way?

3. Upon hearing Peter's story at the end of this text, the church makes a significant change in direction. What values are guiding such a major shift?

4. Think of a major decision made by your congregation. What core values guided that decision?

5. In your experience at your church/ministry, have those values changed over time? If so, how?

Mission

1. What was Peter trying to achieve in this text?

2. What was the church trying to accomplish? Do you think the church's mission changed from the beginning of this text to the end? If so, how? If not, how is the mission consistent?

3. What is your congregation's current mission (do you know the mission statement)?

4. Do you believe your mission has changed over the years? If so, how? Why?

5. Should a church's mission be reviewed and possibly changed if its context changes? Why or why not?

Vision

1. For both Peter and the church in Jerusalem, a major shift occurs regarding who the church ought to include. If the church could now include Gentiles, what do you think is the ultimate vision for the direction of the Jerusalem church?

2. Do you think that inclusivity is part of a divine vision for the church?

3. If your congregation is wildly successful in its mission (as you currently understand its mission), what will this church and/ or the broader community look like in five years? Ten years?

4. Do you consider that to be a legitimate vision for your church?

5. Do you know the current vision statement of your congregation? Has it shaped how you approach your participation in the church's purpose/mission? Should it?

Bibliography

Ansary, Tamim. *Destiny Disrupted: A History of the World through Islamic Eyes.* New York: Public Affairs, 2009.

Border Servant Corps. "Our Mission." https://www.borderservantcorps.org/our-mission-values.

Cherry, Kendra. "What Is Othering?" *Verywell Mind,* May 1, 2023. https://www.verywellmind.com/what-is-othering-5084425.

Clavin, Whitney. "Untangling Quantum Entanglement." *Caltech Magazine,* Fall 2019. https://magazine.caltech.edu/post/untangling-entanglement.

Cush, Denise, et al., eds. *Encyclopedia of Hinduism.* London: Taylor & Francis, 2009.

Duncan, Ligon. "Covenant Theology." *The Gospel Coalition,* 2023. https://www.thegospelcoalition.org/essay/covenant-theology.

"1823: Supreme Court Rules American Indians Do Not Own Land." *Native Voices,* National Institutes of Health, National Library of Medicine. https://www.nlm.nih.gov/nativevoices/timeline/271.html.

Ekman, Paul. "What Is Empathy?" *Greater Good Magazine,* 2023. https://greatergood.berkeley.edu/topic/empathy/definition.

"Empathy." *Psychology Today,* 2023. https://www.psychologytoday.com/us/basics/empathy.

Frakes, Jonathan, dir. "Stardust City Rag." *Star Trek: Picard,* season 1, episode 5. Hollywood, CA: CBS Television Studios, 2020.

Giles, Keith. "Why the World, and the Church, Rejects the Message of Jesus." *Patheos,* July 28, 2023. https://www.patheos.com/blogs/keithgiles/2023/07/why-the-world-and-the-church-rejects-the-message-of-jesus.

Gittins, Anthony J. *Ministry at the Margins: Strategy and Spirituality for Mission.* Maryknoll, NY: Orbis, 2002.

Homolka, Gina. *Skinnytaste One & Done: 140 No-Fuss Dinners for Your Instant Pot, Slow Cooker, Air Fryer, Sheet Pan, Skillet, Dutch Oven & More.* New York: Clarkson Potter, 2018.

King, Martin Luther, Jr. "Read Martin Luther King Jr.'s 'I Have a Dream' Speech in Its Entirety." *Talk of the Nation,* NPR, January 16, 2023. https://www.npr.org/2010/01/18/122701268/i-have-a-dream-speech-in-its-entirety.

Legal Information Institute. "Doctrine of Discovery." Cornell Law School, April 2022. https://www.law.cornell.edu/wex/doctrine_of_discovery.

Live Better Team. "You Can't Have One without the Other: How Body Systems Are Connected." *Revere Health,* August 22, 2016. https://reverehealth.com/live-better/how-body-systems-connected.

Lose, David J. *Making Sense of Scripture: Big Questions About the Book of Faith.* Minneapolis: Augsburg Fortress, 2009.

Lotzof, Kerry. "Are We Made of Stardust?" Natural History Museum of London. https://www.nhm.ac.uk/discover/are-we-really-made-of-stardust.html.

Luther, Martin. "Explanation to the Third Article of the Apostles' Creed." In *Luther's Small Catechism with Evangelical Lutheran Worship Texts.* Minneapolis: Augsburg Fortress, 2006.

Marsden, Francis. "When Was the Bible Finally Canonized?" *Quora.* https://www.quora.com/When-was-the-Bible-finally-canonized.

Native Land Digital. https://native-land.ca.

Newbigin, Lesslie. *The Gospel in a Pluralist Society.* Grand Rapids: Eerdsman, 1989.

"The Nicene Creed." In *Evangelical Lutheran Worship,* by Evangelical Lutheran Church in America. Minneapolis: Fortress, 2006.

Oliver, Erna. "Theology: Still a Queen of Science in the Post-Podern Era." *In die Skriflig/In Luce Verbi* 50:1 (2016). http://dx.doi.org/10.4102/ids.v50i1.2064.

Popkin, Gabriel. "Rising from the Ashes." *Science* 370:6518 (November 13, 2020) 756–59. https://www.science.org/doi/full/10.1126/science.370.6518.756.

Powell, Rachael J. *God's People Made New: How Exploring the Bible Together Launched a Church's Spirit-Filled Future.* Minneapolis: Fortress, 2022.

Preskill, John. "Quantum Entanglement and Quantum Computing." Caltech, News, April 2, 2013. https://www.caltech.edu/about/news/quantum-entanglement-and-quantum-computing-39090.

Sharratt, Michael. *Galileo: Decisive Innovator.* Blackwell Science Biographies. Oxford: Blackwell, 1994.

Wade, Woo. "Rome's Conversion to Christianity and Its Lasting Legacy." Auben Gray Burkhart Coin Collection, Rhodes College, 2023. https://sites.rhodes.edu/coins/romes-conversion-christianity-and-its-lasting-legacy.

www.ingramcontent.com/pod-product-compliance
Lightning Source LLC
Chambersburg PA
CBHW070459090426
42735CB00012B/2614